Elsie's
Turkey Tacos and
Arroz con Pollo

More than 100 Latin-Flavored, Great-Tasting Recipes for Working Moms

ELSIE RAMOS

with Arlen Gargagliano

BICENTENNIAL
1807
WILEY
2007
BICENTENNIAL

WILEY PUBLISHING, INC.

Published by John Wiley & Sons, Inc., Hoboken, New Jersey
Published simultaneously in Canada

For general information on our other products and services or for technical support, please contact our Customer Care Department within the United States at (800) 762-2974, outside the United States at (317) 572-3993 or fax (317) 572-4002.

Wiley also publishes its books in a variety of electronic formats. Some content that appears in print may not be available in electronic books. For more information about Wiley products, visit our web site at www.wiley.com.

Library of Congress Cataloging-in-Publication Data:

Ramos, Elsie.
  Elsie's turkey tacos and arroz con pollo : more than 100 Latin-flavored, great-tasting recipes for working moms / Elsie Ramos.
      p. cm.
  Includes index.
  ISBN-13: 978-0-470-05122-1 (pbk.)
  1. Cookery, Puerto Rican. 2. Cookery, Latin American. 3. Quick and easy cookery. I. Title.
  TX716.P8R36 2007
  641.57295—dc22

                        2006036931

Printed in the United States of America

10 9 8 7 6 5 4 3 2 1

Contents

Dedication

To my sons, Eric, Mark, and Nicholas, who gave me a purpose and a reason to climb as high as I could. You've always been good boys, and for that I thank God.

To Ray, my soulmate, and friend. My luck has changed since we found each other again. Thank you for your patience and for giving my boys and me your boys: David, Shawn, and Nicky.

Para Mami, que sin tu amor y entendimiento de todos mis errores no pudiera continuar con mi vida y llegar donde estoy hoy. ¡Te quiero mucho, Melin!

To my siblings, Mary, Jay, Linda, and Melissa. Thanks for the support and for being proud of me. It wasn't always easy being the middle child or the first to leave the nest. I'm glad I changed my ways!

I love you Jill, Evan, Sean, Daniel, Benny, Elyse, Ariana, Liana, and Armand!

To my Tía Paulina (Pabin). I know you're in heaven just saying "I knew you could do it!" You were right Tía; I am lucky! We miss you.

To my managers, Neal and Jenny. Thank you for allowing me to take the time off and for all the support during the show and the book.

To Justin, thank you for appreciating my "realness" and for introducing me to Stacey.

A special thank you to Arlen, who kept me calm throughout the process and who cared about getting to really know me!

Preface

It's 5:30 on a Tuesday night, and just like every other weeknight, I'm rushing home to New Jersey after working a full day in Manhattan. The boys, ranging in age from seventeen to twenty-two, anxiously await my arrival. Though I'm not sure what I'll be whipping up for dinner, I do know that when I walk through the front door—sometimes even before I get hello hugs—I'll be asked one question: What's for dinner, Mom? I also know that from the moment I enter, just as when my children were much, much younger, I've got less than an hour to get everything ready so that Ray and I—and the boys—can sit down and eat together. As I gaze out the window, I conjure up a mental picture of my pantry and fridge and attempt to take inventory. In the pantry I know I'll find boxes of penne pasta; in the fridge I've got my sofrito (a kind of Puerto Rican relish, and a key ingredient in many of my dishes), some sausage links, and lemon vinaigrette. And now I know what I'll make for dinner: penne with sausage—my way!

Elsie's Turkey Tacos and Arroz con Pollo presents you with my collection of tried and true recipes. These recipes, like my chicken soup that drew national attention during my 2005 participation in Gordon Ramsay's hit reality television show *Hell's Kitchen*, are easy to prepare, no-fuss, tasty home-cooked meals. (Even Chef Ramsay—who was as tough as nails with all of us on *Hell's Kitchen*—enjoyed my food and complimented me in front of everyone!) Though I didn't win the competition, the show—which I participated in after acting on the encouragement of friends and family members—reminded me that food is such an important focus of my life. Participating in *Hell's Kitchen*—and being one of the four finalists—reaffirmed the fact that I've got a great collection of recipes, and that it's time to share them with everyone.

As is the case with many Puerto Ricans, I grew up with two very strong influences: food and family. These two elements are inextricably intertwined in my life—and have led to my great love and appreciation of both. Both of my parents were born in Puerto Rico and came to New York as teenagers. I grew up with four siblings and a large extended family in *El Barrio*, New York City's Upper East Side neighborhood that in so many ways functions as an extension of the island most of its residents came from. Just a walk down the block showers visitors with Puerto Rican–style Spanish, and the welcoming aromas of the food that means home to so many of us. Even Cuchifritos—the store where Mami would take me for special treats like *bacalaítos* (codfish fritters) still sits on 116th Street!

When I was a little girl, Mami and my aunts spent hours in the kitchen, laughing and cooking together. Whether they were making a classic Christmastime dinner of *pernil* (pork shoulder seasoned with adobo, garlic, oregano, and other spices), or a small afternoon snack like *alcapurrias* (meat-stuffed plantain fritters) or *tostones* (green plantain chips), the food was always tasty and the conversation lively! As soon as I got old enough to help out (probably around twelve years old), they included me in their group and I was allowed to help prepare the fritters and clean the beans, all the time being enveloped by the rich aromas that blessed our kitchen. It was there in *la cocina de Mami* (Mom's kitchen) that I learned the secrets of Puerto Rican cooking: use lots of flavor (in the form of sofrito, sazón, and adobo), lots of plantains, and lots of love!

My own recipes were developed out of necessity and desire. I became a single mother at the age of twenty-five with three boys (a set of twins and an infant) and had to work full time, but wanted to keep my meals as nurturing as possible with what little we had. I became quite creative and resourceful, drawing on the tastes I grew up with, and the groceries I could afford. In those days, it was all about the meals.

My culinary repertoire was additionally enhanced as an adult when I went to my parents' home turf; when my twins were just four years old, I spent a year and a half in Puerto Rico. I still vividly remember the delicious morning aromas of cilantro and sofrito as I walked down the street. (Women cooked their rice and beans early so that the kids would be welcomed with a tasty meal when they came home after school.) I also learned that the families I met, no matter how small, cooked more *"por si acaso aparece una visita"* (just in case someone stopped by). Maybe this why I am always prepared to have company over! Being ready to feed family and friends is clearly a personal—and familial—priority.

Still today, my boys—who now tower over me—know that as soon as I walk in the door at night my first questions will be, "Did you eat yet? What did you eat?" Only these days, there are more boys in my house! My partner, Ray, who has three boys of his own, became part of my life and suddenly there were many more of us to cook for. Being a mother of six boys has taught me many, many things. One thing is for sure: when boys are hungry—especially as teens—there had better be food on the table and in the fridge. Cranky teens—of either sex—are certainly no fun. Also, variety is important; repetition can get tedious for anyone. In addition, I strived for flavors that were appealing and comforting. After all, no one likes to have his or her food rejected! So I built on tastes I knew they enjoyed.

Now my boys are getting older, and are not always home for dinner. Still, my kitchen remains the "family" kitchen: my kids, my sisters, brother, and their families know they can count on me for putting out a meal for about twenty on just about every Saturday night. We still laugh and cook together, and though we try not to spend hours and hours in the kitchen, we enjoy the company—and the results. In the end, as much as *I* know I cook well, it always makes me smile to have people love what I've cooked.

Elsie's Turkey Tacos and Arroz con Pollo reflects my family's favorites, the ones that they ask me for again and again. Though some dishes may take longer than others, I promise you that they're all tasty and worth the effort. Also, in time, you'll become more comfortable with them, find your own favorites, adjust them according to your taste, and make them your own! Enjoy—and I hope that these recipes will make you as happy as they've made us.

Introduction

Ramos's Kitchen Rules

Most of my cooking habits have grown out of my wanting to do it all and still have time for myself. My goal is to always get dinner cooked and on the table as soon after I arrive from work as possible. In fact, my number one rule for cooking dinner is never to be in the kitchen cooking past 7 pm (I arrive at home at 5:30). This has driven me to be pretty organized because as much as I love cooking and feeding Ray and the boys, I also want to be able to enjoy my evenings. So when I get home, I park my bag, shout hello, head to the kitchen to turn on my music (smooth jazz during the week, salsa on the weekends), and pour myself a glass of wine (a nice cabernet or merlot); these two things (the music and the wine) are also very important components of my cooking routine!

There are several rules that I follow that relate to my shopping and cooking habits, and I think that these tips will help to guide you. Tried and true, these practical hints are guaranteed to enhance your kitchen time and pleasure.

Plan Ahead for the Week

Sunday is my primary food shopping day; I try to buy for as much of the week as possible at one shot. (It's really the only day when I can take my time.) But even before I go shopping, I am prepared. Here are some simple steps you can take to help you plan for dinners in the week ahead. First, survey your refrigerator, freezer, and pantry to see what you have on hand and what could be paired with what you already have handy. Second, check the store circulars to see what's on sale. If you're like me and have several mouths to feed (and a limited budget!), then you know that the price difference between something on sale and something that's not can be quite large. (I even take my local supermarket circular on the bus with me when I head to my job—and circle items on sale that I can work with.) Also, always keep a supply of rice and beans—and seasonings—so that you can "beef up" and complement any meal you make. Then, adding meat and fresh vegetables is easy.

Buy Precut or Precooked

As you'll see from most of my recipes, I'm a fan of "pre" anything. Of course, I'm certainly not against using fresh—and would recommend it if you have the time—but if you don't, try buying things like:

- frozen, precooked shrimp (or uncooked but peeled and cleaned)
- frozen green beans (instead of the ones you need to trim and cut)
- frozen corn on the cob
- frozen precut peppers
- frozen precut onions
- precut baby carrots
- presliced mushrooms
- packets (or jars) of peeled garlic
- bags of cut lettuce

Buy Large

Whether you're cooking for two or six, it's best to buy larger quantities. This saves time in two different ways. First, buying in bulk will prevent you from needing to take that extra trip to the market. Second, when cooking from this book, you can double the recipe and reheat it on another (leftovers) night or sometimes freeze the extras. Also, buying in larger quantities can be cheaper than buying in smaller packages. If you buy the larger family-size packets of meat and chicken, you can use a portion of them and then freeze what you're not using immediately, so that you have it on hand for another occasion. You should also buy the larger containers of sugar, salt, and oil; again, this will save you money—and time. And don't forget to check the sales; many times stores will offer discounts on larger quantities of cans of vegetables—and that's the time to stock up!

Make Sure You're Always Ready with Sazón and Adobo

Sazón and adobo, traditional Puerto Rican seasonings, are essential in preparing many of my recipes. Sazón is great for both color and flavor; adobo adds the perfect *sabor* (taste). Keep both of these spice blends on hand; it will save you time, energy, and the aggravation of having to measure seasonings every time you cook.

Preseason Your Meats

I highly recommend seasoning meats prior to storing them in the freezer. Having the meat preseasoned makes for not only ease of preparation, but also great-tasting meals. So here's the tip: Keep plenty of resealable, freezable storage bags on hand. Storage bags are easy to handle, and they save freezer space. As soon as you get home from the market, set aside the meat you're going to freeze. Rub it with a layer of Sazón (page 163), Adobo (page 164), or marinade. Then seal the meat in storage bags and place in the freezer. Thaw your frozen meat when you're ready to use it. It's safest to let meat thaw overnight in the refrigerator, especially when the weather is warm. If I forget to do that, I'll place the meat in a large covered pot (no need to add any liquid; as the meat starts to thaw, the steam creates a broth) and let it simmer over a low heat just for a bit to get the frost out. At that point, the meat will feel softer to the touch. Then I cook it as usual.

Always Keep Onion and Garlic Nearby

Always, always have these two on hand. If you run out of your Sofrito (page 158), garlic and onion can certainly lend seasoning help. Onions can also help save a rice or bean dish that you've accidentally overcooked—or even lightly burned. In the case of lightly burned rice, peel an onion, slice it in half, and bury the onion deep into the rice. Cover the pot and let it sit off the heat, for between 10 and 15 minutes. The steam of the rice combined with the flavor of the onion will get rid of the burned taste. You can do the same with a pot of overcooked beans.

Onion and garlic can also help when you precook meat for grilling: before you grill ribs or chicken, bring a big pot of water to boil and add half a peeled onion and several peeled cloves of garlic. Add the meat and cook until the water evaporates about halfway down the pot. For ribs, cook them in boiling water until they're pretty much cooked through (no longer pink), about 35 minutes (and you'll see how they're so tender that the meat will practically fall off the bone after grilling). Chicken requires less time; boil it until it's no longer pink, about 15 minutes. In both cases, as the water evaporates, the flavors of the onion and garlic intensify, so you're adding flavor as well as cutting down on grilling time!

Keep It Convenient

If you have your seasonings handy, you'll save searching time. Keep your adobo, sazón, salt, and pepper front and center. Also when you purchase a large container of oil, transfer it to a more convenient smaller bottle that you can keep close by. Sugar should be nearby, too. In fact, if your sauce seems too salty, sugar can save the day; simply add a bit, taste, and you'll see how the sugar balances out the flavors. In addition to keeping your seasonings handy, you should also keep your favorite utensils nearby. My butcher's knife, *pilón* (small wooden bowl for crushing garlic and herbs), and tongs are always close at hand. In addition, I have a drawer within reaching distance that is filled with all my necessary gadgets, and a nearby cabinet with one of my favorite cooking tools: my caldero, a heavy pot traditionally used in Puerto Rico and other parts of Latin America to cook rice. Microwave containers (and their covers!) should also be somewhat handy; these are great for storing leftovers and, of course, for reheating them in the microwave.

Aluminum Foil is Not Just for Wrapping

Rice is one of the key components of so many of my meals. Since my family makes it so often, we have our own tricks that help us along; one of these has to do with using a cover in addition to the rice pot cover. Next time you make rice, try "sealing" the pot with a sheet of foil under the cover. My mother, sisters, and I all find that if you do this, it decreases the total cooking time. (My sister Mary says that her Dominican friend uses a sheet of paper towels if she doesn't have foil; she claims it creates almost a pressure-cooking situation because it stops the steam from escaping.)

You can also use foil for steaming vegetables. Preheat the oven to 325°F. Place the cut-up vegetables in the center of a piece of foil, fold it over and close the edges (so you've created a kind of pocket), and bake them until steamed but not overcooked, about 15 minutes. When you're ready to serve the veggies, you can discard the foil without worrying about another pot to clean!

Clean As You Go

Nothing irritates me more than a messy kitchen—especially when I'm cooking. So here's the tip: In between a stir or taste, clean up the space around you. If you have limited space—as I do—you'll quickly see that having a clean working kitchen is so much more efficient. And once you start this habit, it's easy to continue. Besides, if you don't do this, it only creates more work for you at the end of the meal!

Soups and Stews

Soups and stews represent three things to me: love, comfort, and simplicity. The love comes from the idea of having someone spend time laboring over glorious vegetables, fabulous meats, and of course the added Puerto Rican touches of sofrito and cilantro, as well as plantains, *calabaza* (pumpkin), and other wonderful components of my traditional cooking. Of course, I also enjoy the preparation of these dishes, and the anticipation that my soups and stews will be enjoyed as they're consumed! The comfort comes from not only the enticing aromas, but also the rich flavors (which I have the habit of topping off with my favorite hot sauce). The simplicity is the whole one-pot feature of these dishes; it's great to be able to combine ingredients that enhance each other and work together to create dishes with richness and depth.

Whether it's a damp and chilly autumn day, an ice-cold wintry day, one of those slushy spring days, or an unusually brisk summer day, a soup or stew is a welcome dish. I hope that this collection will bring you and your family the joy that this collection has brought my family and me!

My Famous Chicken Soup

Everyone who tries this soup just loves it! It's very simple to prepare, and the cilantro and plantains make it incredibly tasty. In fact, your family will love it so much that you might want to double the recipe and freeze half for another time. Traditionally my mom seasoned this soup with the rich flavor of pork neck bones; I'm using cooked ham, which is slightly different but just as good. My family especially likes this soup with Garlic Bread (page 172) and a large leafy green salad.

SERVES 6

One 3-pound whole chicken, cut up, or 3 pounds chicken drumsticks and thighs

3 garlic cloves, peeled and chopped

2 very ripe plantains (almost black)

1 pound cooked ham, cut into $1/4$-inch cubes

$1/4$ cup chopped fresh cilantro leaves

2 teaspoons Sazón (page 163)

1 chicken bouillon cube

Salt

1 In a stockpot, combine the chicken, garlic, and enough water to cover by about 1 inch. Stir well. Cover and cook over medium heat until the chicken is no longer pink, about 25 minutes, adding more water if it seems to be evaporating too quickly (the water level should always cover the chicken).

2 While the chicken is simmering, prepare the plantains: Cut the ends off and cut a slit lengthwise down the middle. Open and remove the peel, using a knife or your hands, as if you were taking a jacket off somebody. Cut the plantain into $1/2$-inch chunks and transfer to a bowl. Using a potato masher, smash the plantain chunks until they have a consistency similar to mashed potatoes. Spoon some into your hands, form about 10 to 12 little meatball shapes about 1 inch in diameter (though they'll be much stickier than meatballs and certainly not perfectly shaped!), and set aside.

3 Add the ham, cilantro, and sazón to the stockpot and mix. Pour in 2 more cups water (less if it's getting close to the top; you have to allow room for the plantains). Bring the soup to a boil, and add the plantain balls and the bouillon cube. Let boil until the plantains are cooked, stirring occasionally, about 10 minutes.

4 Add salt to taste and serve immediately, or let cool, transfer to a large container, cover, and refridgerate for up to 3 days or freeze for up to 6 months.

Pollo Guisado   *Chicken Stew*

The first meal Ray ever cooked for me was "his" version of *pollo guisado*. Though his intentions were great, and he tried to emulate Mom's recipe, he ended up making mostly just *pollo*. So my mom got her hands on it, added her special *toque* (touch), and it became the delicious and hearty dish we make today. Served by itself, or with rice and a crusty loaf of Garlic Bread (page 172), this makes a terrific meal on a damp and chilly afternoon.

SERVES 4 TO 6

6 to 8 chicken pieces (2 to $2^{1}/_{2}$ pounds), preferably drumsticks and thighs, excess skin removed

2 tablespoons Sofrito (page 158)

One 8-ounce can tomato sauce

1 tablespoon Sazón (page 163)

4 carrots, peeled and diced into bite-size chunks

3 russet potatoes, peeled and diced into bite-size chunks

4 to 6 small half-ears fresh corn, husks and silk removed, or thawed frozen

Salt and freshly ground black pepper

$^{1}/_{4}$ cup chopped fresh cilantro leaves

1 Place the chicken in a *caldero* or heavy pot. Using a spoon or your hands, coat the chicken pieces with the sofrito. Cover and cook over medium heat, stirring from time to time to prevent sticking (you don't need to add water because the steam creates a broth), until the meat is no longer pink, 15 or 20 minutes.

2 Add the tomato sauce and sazón and mix well. Let the chicken simmer over low heat, stirring occasionally, until the tomato sauce starts to bubble, about 5 minutes. Remove any loose chicken skin.

3 Add the carrots, potatoes, corn (if using frozen, wait another 5 minutes; otherwise it will get too mushy) and 2 to 3 cups water, enough to cover the vegetables. Raise the heat and bring the stew to a boil. Simmer uncovered, stirring occasionally and skimming fat as needed, until the vegetables become tender, about 10 minutes.

4 Add salt and pepper to taste, sprinkle the cilantro on top, and serve.

Caldo de Pollo *Chicken Broth*

It seemed like every New Year's Day, as we sat around nursing headaches from the long night's cele-bration, Mami would say, *"¡Vamos a preparar un caldo de pollo!"* (Let's make chicken broth!) Though chicken broth is usually a base for many dishes, in my house we've always served it on its own as a delicious medicine. Whenever someone was coming down with a cold—or after a big celebration the night before—this magic, light soup would be the cure. According to my mom and her sisters, each of the ingredients has a specific reason for being there: The chicken is the base, the garlic is good for the stomach, the *salchichón* (sausage) adds spice, and the cilantro adds flavor. The combination of fla-vors is unbelievable, and I serve this with fresh Tostones (page 74) even when we're all well!

SERVES 6

1 teaspoon unsalted butter (optional)

2$^1/_2$ pounds chicken pieces, preferably drumsticks and thighs

Salt and freshly ground black pepper

Garlic powder

$^1/_2$ cup diced salchichón or hard salami, cut into $^1/_4$-inch cubes

2 or 3 whole cilantro sprigs, including the leaves

2 or 3 garlic cloves, peeled

1 chicken bouillon cube

1 In a large nonstick frying pan (a nonstick pan is best because this way the chicken skin won't stick, but if you don't have a nonstick pan, just melt a teaspoon of butter in the bottom of the pan), place the chicken pieces so they're flat, skin side down. Season with a dash of salt, pepper, and garlic powder. Cover the pot and cook over low heat, turning occasionally, until the chicken is no longer pink, 15 to 20 minutes.

2 Uncover and add the salchichón, cilantro, and garlic cloves. You'll notice some liquid in the pan as a result of the steam, so stir to mix everything together. Cover and simmer over low heat until the garlic is tender, another 10 to 15 minutes.

3 Pour in 2 cups water, add the bouillon cube, and raise the heat to medium. Bring the broth to a boil, and let simmer until the chicken is cooked through, about 10 minutes more.

4 Serve the broth (without the other ingredients) in a bowl or cup. You can serve the solids over rice. You can also serve this dish as a soup with all the ingredients.

Melin's Sensational Sancocho *Pork and Vegetable Stew*

My mom—known throughout her childhood (and by most of my older relatives) as Melin—is great at making many meals, but when we were kids, her best dish was her *sancocho*. In fact, as my sisters and brother and I started heading in our separate ways, it was Mami's sancocho that would bring us all home for dinner together on a Saturday night. This Puerto Rican–style stew, richly flavored by the pork neck bones and sofrito and packed with Caribbean vegetables like the nutty-flavored yet potato-like *yautía*, is a lot of work, but definitely worth the effort. I usually double this recipe so that we can enjoy it for several days.

SERVES 6

2 green plantains

5 medium size green bananas,

6 pounds pork neck bones (see Note)

2 tablespoons Sofrito (page 158)

1 teaspoon Sazón (page 163)

2 medium yautía (malanga), peeled and diced into bite-size chunks (see Note)

2 russet potatoes, peeled and diced

$^1/_2$ pound *calabaza* (green or West Indian pumpkin), peeled and diced into bite-size chunks (see Note)

3 carrots, peeled and diced into bite-size chunks

8 half-ears fresh corn, husks and silk removed, or thawed frozen

1 Soak the plantains and green bananas in warm water in a large bowl or in the sink for about 20 minutes; this will soften the skin and make peeling easier. Remove from the water, dry them, cut the ends off, and cut a slit lengthwise down the skin. Open the peel, using a knife or your hands, as if you were taking a jacket off somebody. Cut the plantains and bananas on the diagonal into $^1/_2$-inch chunks and set aside.

2 In a stockpot, combine the pork neck bones and enough water to cover them by about 3 inches, and bring to a boil. Stir in the sofrito and sazón. Once the water boils again, cook until the pork neck bones brown, and the skin softens, about 20 minutes

3 Stir in the yautía, potatoes, calabaza, carrots, and corn (if using frozen, wait another 5 minutes; otherwise it will get too mushy). Simmer uncovered over medium heat, stirring occasionally, until the vegetables become tender, about 15 minutes. Serve immediately.

NOTE: Pork neck bones, yautía, and calabaza are available in Latin American and West Indian groceries, as well as some larger supermarkets.

Patitas de Puerco *Pigs' Feet Stew*

Please don't be put off by the name; this dish is so delicious. If you've never eaten or made pigs' feet stew before, you're in for a treat! The first time I prepared this and served it at dinner, in the midst of devouring it my boys said, "Mom, this is great! What is it?" They were five and ten years old at the time, and I knew that the idea of eating pigs' feet would put them off—so I fibbed. "It's chicken, guys! Enjoy!" They smiled and went on to have seconds. (Years later I did confess, but by then they loved the stew so much that they didn't care!) Serve it by itself, or over a bed of rice, which mixes beautifully with the sauce.

SERVES 6

2 pounds salted pigs' feet (see Note), submerged in a large pot of water (at room temperature) for an hour to remove excess salt, and then drained

One 15- to 16-ounce can garbanzo beans (chickpeas), drained

2 large russet potatoes, peeled and diced into bite-size chunks

One 8-ounce can tomato sauce

1 tablespoon Sofrito (page 158)

1 tablespoon Sazón (page 163)

1 Place the pigs' feet in a large *caldero* or heavy pot. Cover them with water by about 2 inches and bring to a boil. Cook at a steady slow boil until the meat becomes tender, about 2 hours, adding water as frequently as needed. (Pigs' feet are very tough, so boiling them for a long time will soften them up.)

2 Once the pigs' feet have reached the consistency you like, add the garbanzo beans, potatoes, tomato sauce, sofrito, and sazón and stir well. Cover and cook over low heat, stirring once in a while, until the potatoes are soft, 20 to 30 minutes. Serve immediately.

NOTE: Salted pigs' feet are available in Latin American and West Indian groceries, as well as some larger butchers.

Orejitas Guisadas   *Pig's Ear Stew*

In our culture, we cook it all! If you've never heard of cooking—or eating—pigs' ears, this will sound quite foreign. However, to my parents and the many people who frequent the Cuchifritos store in El Barrio (Spanish Harlem), this dish is a delicacy. So put away your preconceived notions and try this because it's *delicioso*! Serve with Basic White Rice (page 171).

SERVES 4

1¹/₂ pounds *orejitas* (pigs' ears), cut into bite-size pieces (see Note)

1 small onion, peeled and coarsely chopped

1 small tomato, coarsely chopped

¹/₄ cup ketchup (yes, ketchup!)

1 teaspoon Sofrito (page 158)

1 teaspoon Sazón (page 163)

Tabasco sauce

1 Place the pigs' ears in a large pot of water, add enough water to cover them by at least 2 inches, and bring to a boil. Cook at a steady slow boil over medium heat until the meat starts to soften (though they never get completely soft), about 2 hours, adding water as needed to keep the meat covered. Drain and set aside.

2 In a large saucepan over low heat, combine the orejitas with the onion and tomato. Mix well. Stir in the ketchup, sofrito, and sazón. Cook over low heat, stirring frequently, until the sauce begins to softly boil and the onions soften, about 5 minutes. Add a dash of Tabasco and serve.

NOTE: Pigs' ears are available in Latin American and West Indian groceries, as well as some larger butchers.

Carne Guisada *Beef Stew*

My mother was just a teenager when she arrived in New York. Though she was surrounded by many others from Puerto Rico, since she loved to cook she started adopting—and adapting—dishes she saw or heard about in New York. The sofrito and cilantro are the touches that Mami added to make this stew more appealing to her and her family. This one, in which she cooked the meat for hours in order to make it tender, was one of my father's favorites. Now I've added my own secret ingredient to make it one of my family's favorites! Enjoy this stew with Arroz con Maíz (page 93) and a leafy green salad.

SERVES 6

2 tablespoons vegetable oil

2 pounds stew beef chunks, cut into bite-size chunks

2 tablespoons Sofrito (page 158)

2 tablespoons My Best Barbecue Sauce (page 168)
   or a jarred barbecue sauce (secret's out!)

2 teaspoons tomato paste

1 or 2 fresh cilantro sprigs, including the leaves

2 large russet potatoes, peeled and cut into bite-size chunks

3 or 4 whole carrots, peeled and cut into bite-size chunks

1 Heat the oil in a large *caldero* or heavy pot. Add the beef and sofrito and mix well to coat.

2 Cover and cook over low heat, stirring occasionally, until the beef has browned, about 30 minutes.

3 Stir in the barbecue sauce, tomato paste, and cilantro. Mix well. Cover again, and cook until the meat is slightly tender, about 1 hour.

4 Add the potatoes and carrots, along with 2 cups water, and stir to combine. Raise the heat and bring to a boil. Stir, reduce the heat, cover, and simmer until the vegetables are tender, another 20 to 30 minutes. Serve immediately.

Cola de Res *Oxtail Stew*

The aroma of this stew, like its flavor, is deliciously rich. Made with the tail of an ox (or maybe the tail of a steer), this was one of those dishes that couldn't be exactly described in terms of ingredients to my sons. But luckily, I didn't need to; one whiff won them over! The first time I watched Mami prepare this dish it seemed like a lot of work. However, I encourage you to try it because it's certainly worth the effort. Also, you might want to double this recipe (since you are taking the time to make it) and freeze half for another day. Serve this stew with Basic White Rice (page 171), Garlic Bread (page 172), and a leafy green salad.

SERVES 6

2 pounds oxtails, cut into 2-inch chunks and trimmed of excess fat

One 8-ounce can tomato sauce

1/4 cup chopped fresh cilantro leaves

2 tablespoons Sofrito (page 158)

1 teaspoon Sazón (page 163)

2 medium russet potatoes, peeled and cut into 1-inch cubes

1 Rinse the oxtails and put them into a large *caldero* or heavy pot. Add enough water to cover them by about 1 inch. Raise the heat to high and bring to a boil. Reduce the heat and let them cook uncovered until the meat is tender, about 1 hour. Turn off the heat, but leave the meat in the water.

2 Once slightly cooled, use a spoon or ladle to skim the fat from the top of the water (you don't have to get it all; some left over is fine, but remove as much as you can).

3 Add the tomato sauce, cilantro, sofrito, and sazón. Reduce the heat to medium, add the potatoes, and continue cooking until they're tender, about 10 minutes more. Serve hot.

Sopa de Camarones *Shrimp Soup*

This is one of the most delicious and comforting soups to me and my siblings. Even today, my sisters and brother and I will sometimes split the cost of a couple of pounds of shrimp and bring them over to Mami in Manhattan so that she can make us our favorite *sopa*! You can enjoy this soup any time of year, but I think it's best in the winter. Though Mami bought her shrimp fresh and whole, if you buy cleaned and cooked (or uncooked) shrimp, it will save you both time and aggravation. Serve with a leafy green salad topped with Elsie's Lemon Vinaigrette (page 161).

SERVES 6

$^1/_2$ cup long-grain white rice

One 8-ounce can tomato sauce

One 7- or 8-ounce jar roasted peppers, drained and
  coarsely chopped

$^1/_3$ cup chopped fresh cilantro leaves

1 tablespoon Sofrito (page 158)

3 large russet potatoes, peeled and cut into 1-inch cubes

2 pounds peeled, deveined, and cooked medium shrimp
  (thawed if frozen)

Tabasco sauce

1 In a small saucepan, bring 1 cup water to boil. Stir in the rice, reduce the heat to low, and cover. Simmer until cooked, about 20 minutes.

2 Meanwhile, fill a large soup or stockpot half way with water (about $4^1/_2$ quarts) and bring it to a boil. Add the tomato sauce, peppers, cilantro, and sofrito and stir well. Reduce the heat to medium. Add the potatoes and let simmer until they start to soften, about 10 minutes.

3 Add the shrimp, stir well, and continue cooking just until heated through. Add Tabasco to taste.

4 Pour the soup into individual serving bowls, add a spoonful of rice to each one, and serve.

Guisado de Sardina con Cebolla *Sardine and Onion Stew*

When the five of us finally grew up and left home, Mami began cooking for one. It was initially quite tough for her to do; it's sometimes hard to scale down dishes after making them for a small crowd for so many years. I remember visiting her one day when she was happily enjoying her stew of small fish, topped with her favorite white rice. I asked her if it was okay. She immediately responded, *"¡Sí muchacha—este guisado está delicioso!"* (This stew is delicious!). Honestly, I didn't believe it until I tried it; it was really good! (God bless Mami—who still knows how to turn just about anything into an enjoyable meal!) This is clearly an adult dish (unless your kids—unlike mine—are fond of sardines), that is perfect served atop a few spoonfuls of Basic White Rice (page 171).

SERVES 2

1 teaspoon extra virgin olive oil

One 15- to 16-ounce can boneless sardines, drained

1 small onion, peeled and sliced into thin rings

1 tablespoon tomato sauce

1 teaspoon ketchup

Heat the oil in a skillet over low heat. Add the sardines, onion, tomato sauce, and ketchup and mix well. Cover and simmer, stirring occasionally, until heated through, about 10 minutes. Serve over white rice.

Bacalao Guisado   *Codfish Stew*

Bacalao Guisado has long been one of Mami's and my favorite dishes. Puerto Ricans, like many of their fellow Caribes, know the ease of preparation and tastiness of their most ubiquitous fish: cod. For years my boys wouldn't eat this dish because they were afraid of getting a fish bone stuck in their throat. (This was because every time my family made bacalao together, when we sat down to eat, you could hear all the grown-ups saying: *"Cuidado con los huesos,"* which means watch out for the bones; Mami still says this!) These days I use boneless cod, and my boys are now grown up enough to realize how tasty and delicious this stew is with a bowl of rice and a salad. I like this stew because I can keep it in my fridge for up to five days—though usually, with my gang, it's long gone before then.

SERVES 6

2^1/$_2$ pounds boneless dried codfish

2 tablespoons vegetable oil

2 to 3 small Spanish onions, peeled and
  sliced into ^{1}/$_4$-inch-thick rings

1 large red bell pepper, seeded and julienned
  (sliced into ^{1}/$_8$-inch-thick, 1-inch-long strips)

1 large green pepper, seeded and julienned
  (sliced into ^{1}/$_8$-inch-thick, 1-inch-long strips)

One 8-ounce can tomato sauce

1 large tomato, diced into bite-size chunks

1 tablespoon Sazón (page 163)

1 Place the codfish in a large pot. Add enough water to cover it and let it soak for about 1 hour to remove some of the salt. After an hour, discard the water and refill with clean water. Bring the pot to a boil and cook until the fish is not too salty, about 10 minutes. (Taste a piece and you'll know right away if it's still too salty!) If it's fine, drain it and let it cool, otherwise give it another 10 minutes to soak, off the heat, before draining. When it's cool enough to handle, shred it into bite-size pieces using your fingers or a fork. Set it aside.

2 Meanwhile, heat the oil in a large skillet over medium heat. Add the onions and peppers and cook, stirring often, until they start to soften, about 2 minutes. Add the tomato sauce, cover, and cook, stirring frequently, until the onions are transparent, about 5 minutes. Stir in the tomato and reduce the heat to low. Cook until it reaches a soft boil, about 10 minutes.

3 Stir the shredded codfish and the sazón into the onion mixture. Cover and cook over low heat, stirring frequently, until heated through, 8 to 10 minutes.

4 Serve immediately, or cover and refrigerate for up to 5 days and reheat just before serving.

Guisado de Berenjena y Bacalao *Eggplant and Codfish Stew*

Before I combined eggplant with codfish, I had underestimated it! Because of its almost sweet taste and luscious texture, not to mention its ability to cook quickly (something I'm always looking for!), this dish easily became incorporated into my repertoire. Though it may have been somewhat new to me, *berenjena* is no stranger to Puerto Rican cooking. Actually, it fits nicely into a cuisine that's all about richness and intensity of flavor. In addition to being delicious, eggplant also combines beautifully with other foods; in this case, its smoothness marries well with the salted fish. I usually serve this over Basic White Rice (page 171) and with one of my favorite veggies (yuca, green bananas, or green plantains).

SERVES 4

1 pound boneless dried codfish

1 medium eggplant

2 tablespoons extra virgin olive oil

1 red bell pepper, seeded and julienned
(sliced into $1/8$-inch-thick, 1-inch-long strips)

1 green bell pepper, seeded and julienned
(sliced into $1/8$-inch-thick, 1-inch-long strips)

1 medium onion, peeled and sliced into thin rings

2 garlic cloves, peeled and minced

1 Place the codfish in a large pot. Add enough water to cover it and let it soak for about 1 hour to remove some of the salt. After an hour, discard the water and refill with clean water. Bring the pot to a boil and cook until the fish is not too salty, about 10 minutes. (Taste a piece and you'll know right away if it's still too salty!) If it's fine, drain it and let it cool; otherwise give it another 10 minutes to soak, off the heat, before draining. When it's cool enough to handle, shred it into bite-size pieces using your fingers or a fork. Set it aside.

2 Peel and cut the eggplant into 1-inch-thick rounds. Heat $^1/_4$ cup water in a skillet over medium heat. Place the eggplant into the water, and let cook until the eggplant has softened, about 15 minutes. Drain and set aside.

3 In a second shallow pan, heat the oil over low heat. Add the peppers, onion, and garlic and cook, stirring frequently, until the peppers start to soften, about 10 minutes.

4 Stir in the shredded codfish, and immediately add the eggplant. Cover and cook until the eggplant is soft and the mixture starts to simmer, about 15 minutes. Serve immediately.

Sopón de Pescado *Fish Soup*

When Mami was little, this traditional fish soup was quite popular. After the *hombres* would return from a successful fishing trip, they would bring their *mujeres* some of their catch. While the men washed up and enjoyed a couple of drinks, the women would get to work making this fabulous *sopa*. Just as Mami always did, I use the head and tail of the fish to create a flavorful broth (which she also swears has curative powers!) before adding the fresh white chunks of fish. Served topped with a few dashes of Tabasco, or simply with a few spoonfuls of white rice (and Garlic Bread, page 172, and leafy green salad on the side), this soup makes a great lunch or light dinner.

SERVES 6

2 whole white fish (I like kingfish), about 2 pounds, boned and skinned (see Note)

1 small onion, peeled and halved

4 garlic cloves, peeled

2 teaspoons salt

1 teaspoon whole black peppercorns

2 bay leaves

1 tablespoon Adobo (page 164)

1 tablespoon unsalted butter

1. Place the head, tail, skin, and bones of the fish and the onion in a stockpot with 6 quarts water. Add the garlic, salt, pepper, and bay leaves to the pot. Bring to a full boil over high heat and cook until the broth is reduced by half, about 25 minutes. Strain the broth into a clean stockpot and set aside (discard the strained solid ingredients).

2. Dice the fish fillets into 1-inch chunks, place in a bowl, and season with the adobo. Mix so the pieces are well covered.

3. Melt the butter in a medium skillet over medium heat. Add the fish pieces. Cook until the fish is lightly browned on one side, about 5

minutes. Flip and cook the other side until it's lightly browned, about 5 minutes more.

4 Add the fish to the strained broth. Stir and cook over low heat until warmed through, about 5 minutes. Serve immediately.

NOTE: Get the fish cleaned at the fish market, but be sure to keep the heads and tails!

Habichuelas Guisadas *Red Bean Stew*

There are two ingredients in this very tasty dish that may be new to you: The first is pork neck bones, used primarily in the south of the United States and across the Caribbean to flavor soups and stews, and the second is the tropical squash *calabaza*. Also known as the West Indian pumpkin, the skin color varies from tan to green, though the flesh is orange just like the northern pumpkin. This tropical relative of butternut squash is grown throughout the Caribbean and in Central America and South America, has a sweet taste, and marries well with many other flavors.

SERVES 6

1¼ cups dried pink or red kidney beans (half a 1-pound bag)

2 pounds pork neck bones (available in Latin American and West Indian markets)

One 8-ounce can tomato sauce

¼ cup chopped fresh cilantro

1 large russet potato, peeled and diced into bite-size chunks

½ pound *calabaza* (green or West Indian pumpkin), peeled and diced into bite-size chunks

1 teaspoon salt

1 Pour the beans into a strainer. Rinse carefully, removing any dirt or small stones. Transfer to a pot, fill the pot with enough water to cover the beans by about 2 inches of water, and let sit for at least 8 hours or overnight.

2 Drain the water, and refill the pot with enough water to cover the beans by about 2 inches. Add the pork neck bones, stir well, and simmer over medium heat until the beans are tender, about 1 hour; adding water as needed to keep the beans covered.

3 Add the tomato sauce and cilantro and stir well. Add the potatoes and squash, stir, cover, and cook until the vegetables are tender, 10 to 15 minutes. Add salt. Remove the pork neck bones and serve.

Sopa de Gandules *Pigeon Pea Soup*

This *sopa* was—and still is—a very common meal in Puerto Rico. My mother, like many *puertoriqueños*, grew up with *gandules* (pigeon peas) growing in her backyard. Mami said that my *abuela* (grandma) was so resourceful and knew—as I do now—how to feed a large family with what she had. The aroma of the gandules cooking, along with the smell of fresh chopped cilantro, will take any *Boricua* (someone from *Borinquen*, the name given by the indigenous peoples to Puerto Rico) back to his or her native island. Serve with Tostones (page 74).

SERVES 4

2 medium russet potatoes, peeled and cut into eighths

Two 15- to 16-ounce cans gandules (pigeon peas), drained

$^1/_2$ cup diced cooked ham (about $^1/_4$ pound) cut into bite-size chunks

$^1/_2$ cup canned tomato sauce

$^1/_4$ cup chopped fresh cilantro leaves

1 teaspoon Sazón (page 163)

Salt and freshly ground black pepper

Fill a stockpot with 2 quarts water and bring to a boil over high heat. Reduce the heat to medium, add the potatoes, gandules, ham, tomato sauce, cilantro, and sazón and simmer until the potatoes are tender, about 10 minutes. Add salt and pepper to taste and serve.

Guisado de Pitipua *Pea Stew*

I always made fun of this word because it sounded so strange in Puerto Rico, where peas are also called *chícharos*. Mami always referred to them as *pitipua*, which is the Spanish pronunciation of *petits pois*, the French word for peas. (Dominicans also say pitipua.) Though I found the name amusing, I found the stew fascinating! This tasty stew can also be made with red or pink beans.

SERVES 4

One 8-ounce can tomato sauce

2 tablespoons extra virgin olive oil

1 tablespoon Sofrito (page 158)

1 teaspoon Sazón (page 163)

$^1/_2$ pound cooked ham, cut into $^1/_4$-inch cubes

1 pound fresh pound *calabaza* (green or West Indian pumpkin), peeled and diced into bite-size chunks (see Note)

One 15- to 16-ounce can whole green peas (*chícharos* in Spanish), drained

1 In a stockpot, combine the tomato sauce, oil, sofrito, and sazón and cook, covered, over low heat until it begins to simmer, about 5 minutes. Add the ham, stir well, cover again, and let simmer until the tomato sauce begins to softly boil, about 3 minutes.

2 Stir in the calabaza. Mix well and leave uncovered. Stir in 2 cups water and raise the heat to high. Cook, stirring occasionally, until it begins to boil, about 7 minutes.

3 Reduce the heat to medium and continue cooking, stirring from time to time, until the calabaza is very tender, about 10 minutes. Add the peas and continue to cook, stirring occasionally, until heated through, about 5 minutes.

NOTE: Calabaza is available in Latin American and West Indian groceries, as well as some larger supermarkets.

Appetizers and Side Dishes

Appetizers are my favorite part of dinner; they're the introduction to a larger production. They should be delicious, exciting, and appetite-enhancing but not filling, so that everyone has plenty of room to continue the meal—though this has never been an issue in my family! I especially enjoy the socializing that comes with this part of dinner.

Side dishes are similar in that they also should complement the rest of the meal and not compete against it. After all, what's a Puerto Rican dinner without a side of rice, pasta, or *verduras* (vegetables)? Oh, did I mention rice? Luckily we have so many variations that you can't tire of them.

As you go through this section, I hope you'll find many dishes that are new to you, that you'll try them, and that you'll discover (or maybe rediscover) some new favorites.

Salads, Vegetables, and Other Sides

Ensalada de Cangrejo   *Crab Salad*

Having a big family is great, but it means that often I have to make things on the spur of the moment. Because I work full time, I'm always developing recipes depending—of course—on what Mom taught me, but also on what I have in my kitchen. This fast salad is a great example of something that's easily pulled together for lunch or a before-dinner treat. (Besides, you can make huge amounts of this and it's relatively inexpensive.) Serve as a lunch over Basic White Rice (page 171) with Elsie's Spiced-Up Corn (page 46), or as an appetizer, spooned onto crackers.

SERVES 6
(If it's served with rice,
it can be a meal; otherwise,
it's an appetizer or side)

$^1/_3$ cup extra virgin olive oil

$^1/_3$ cup white vinegar, or to taste

One 16-ounce jar roasted red peppers, drained and juice reserved, cut into $^1/_4$-inch thick, $^1/_2$-inch-long strips

2 teaspoons Sazón (page 163)

1 large white onion, peeled and sliced into $^1/_4$-inch-thick rings

One 8-ounce can corn, drained

2 pounds imitation crab meat

1 In a large bowl, combine the oil, vinegar, the juice from the roasted peppers, and the sazón. Add the peppers, onion slices, and corn. Mix well, and set aside.

2 Shred the crab into bite-size pieces. Add to the oil and vinegar mixture. Stir to coat. If the mixture is too dry, add small amounts of vinegar and pepper juice to taste. Serve immediately, or cover and refrigerate for 2 to 3 days.

Ensalada de Bacalao   *Codfish Salad*

This codfish salad was a favorite when Mami wanted to honor the no-meat rule on Fridays during Lent. Even my kids, who didn't know exactly what was in it at first, love it. This delicious seafood salad can be eaten warm or chilled, but the longer it marinates in the fridge, the better it gets! Serve on its own or with Basic White Rice (page 171).

SERVES 6

2 pounds boneless dried codfish

2 tablespoons olive oil

1 large Vidalia onion, peeled and julienned, (sliced into $1/8$-inch-thick, 1-inch-long strips)

1 red bell pepper, seeded and julienned (sliced into $1/8$-inch-thick, 1-inch-long strips)

1 green bell pepper, seeded and julienned (sliced into $1/8$-inch-thick, 1-inch-long strips)

1 large tomato, seeded and diced into bite-size chunks

1 teaspoon white vinegar

1 large russet potato, peeled and cubed

4 large eggs

2 bay leaves

Freshly ground black pepper

1 Place the codfish in a large pot. Add enough water to cover it and let it soak for about 1 hour to remove some of the salt. After an hour, discard the water and refill with clean water. Bring the pot to a boil and cook until the fish is not too salty, about 10 minutes. (Taste a piece and you'll know right away if it's still too salty!) If it's fine, drain it and let it cool; otherwise give it another 10 minutes to soak, off the heat, before draining. When it's cool enough to handle, shred it into bite-size pieces using your fingers or a fork. Set it aside.

2 Heat the oil in a large skillet over medium heat. As soon as it's hot, add the onion, peppers, and tomato and stir well. Cover and cook over low heat, stirring from time to time, until all the vegetables have softened, about 10 minutes. Stir in the vinegar and turn off the heat.

3 Bring a medium pot of water to a boil. Add the potato and the eggs. Cook until the potatoes are tender and the eggs are hard-cooked, about 8 minutes. Drain both. Run under cold water. When the eggs are cool enough to handle, peel and coarsely chop them.

4 In a large bowl, combine the shredded codfish, potatoes, eggs, and vegetable mixture. Add the bay leaves and pepper and mix well. Serve immediately, or cover and chill in the refrigerator for at least an hour, or overnight. Remove the bay leaves before serving.

Ensalada de Salmón *Salmon Salad*

Mami, who was always quick to make cans of tuna into salad for lunch or dinner, also came up with this salmon salad alternate. This salad is so easy and quick; there's absolutely no cooking required—which makes this an ideal meal on steamy summer nights. Serve with Basic White Rice (page 171) and a leafy green salad.

SERVES 4

One 14.75-ounce can salmon, drained, picked over to remove any skin and bones

1 large onion, peeled and coarsely chopped

1 large tomato, coarsely chopped

1 tablespoon extra virgin olive oil

Freshly ground black pepper

Tostones (page 74, you only need half the recipe— 2 or 3 plantains—so you can save the other half for snacking or for guacamole!)

2 tablespoons chopped fresh cilantro leaves

Carefully check the canned salmon for bones; make sure you remove them all. In a medium bowl, combine the salmon, onion, and tomato. Stir well. Add the olive oil and pepper to taste and mix well. Serve immediately, or cover and refrigerate for about 1 hour or until well chilled. Just before serving, place tostones on a serving plate and top with the salmon salad. Sprinkle cilantro on top.

Ensalada de Camarones *Cold Shrimp Salad*

On a hot summer's eve, I look for cooling—as well as simple and satisfying—meals. This could, of course, be made into a side dish or an appetizer, but my family enjoys this as a main course on steamy nights, with a side of Basic White Rice (page 171) and Tostones (page 74).

SERVES 6

$1/2$ cup white vinegar

$1/4$ cup olive oil

1 teaspoon Sazón (page 163)

1 large Vidalia onion, peeled and sliced into thin rings

One 7-ounce jar roasted peppers, drained and diced into bite-size chunks

1 cup Mexican-Style Corn (page 169), one 11-ounce can Mexican-style corn, drained or 1 cup thawed frozen corn

2 pounds peeled, deveined, and cooked medium shrimp (thawed if frozen)

Salt and freshly ground black pepper

1 Bring a large pot of water to a boil.

2 In a large bowl, combine the vinegar, oil, and sazón. Add the onion, peppers, and corn to the dressing. Mix well.

3 Add the shrimp to the boiling water and cook until pink, about 5 minutes. Drain and lay the shrimp on paper towels to drain any excess water.

4 Add the shrimp to the bowl with the oil and vinegar mixture and stir well to coat. Cover and refrigerate for at least 1 hour, or overnight. Add salt and pepper to taste just before serving.

Ensalada de Aguacate y Bacalao *Avocado and Codfish Salad*

I absolutely love avocados; they add such a smooth and cooling flavor to any dish—which is why I really like them in this dish. The codfish is salty on its own, but balances beautifully with the *aguacate*. Sometimes I make this salad as a side just for Ray (who is a big fan of codfish) and me, and then we enjoy it for lunch the following day.

SERVES 4

1 pound boneless dried codfish

2 medium russet potatoes, peeled and cut into $^1/_2$-inch wedges

$^1/_4$ cup finely diced onion

1 small avocado, peeled, pitted, and cut into bite-size chunks

3 hard-cooked eggs, peeled and sliced

Salt and freshly ground black pepper

$^1/_2$ cup extra virgin olive oil

1 Place the codfish in a large pot. Add enough water to cover it and let it soak for about 1 hour to remove some of the salt. After an hour, discard the water and refill with clean water. Bring the pot to a boil and cook until the fish is not too salty, about 10 minutes. (Taste a piece and you'll know right away if it's still too salty!) If it's fine, drain it and let it cool; otherwise give it another 10 minutes to soak, off the heat, before draining. When it's cool enough to handle, shred it into bite-size pieces using your fingers or a fork. Set it aside.

2 Fill a medium saucepan with water, add the potatoes, and bring to a boil. Cook the potatoes until tender, about 10 minutes. Drain and let cool.

3 Place the potatoes, onion, and avocado in a large serving bowl. Add the codfish and toss to combine. Place the sliced egg on top, and lightly season with salt and pepper. Drizzle with oil and serve.

Ensalada de Papaya *Papaya Salad*

My Tía Lydia told me that papaya cures you of "simple ailments," or illnesses that aren't too serious. After hearing a doctor's suggestion that she take antibiotics, Tía would run to the *Chinitos*, as she affectionately called the Korean grocer on the corner, and pick up some papaya instead. Obviously that worked for her. This salad was taught to me by Aunt Lydia after she enjoyed it while visiting friends in Aruba! (Go Tía!) Though she enjoyed this without dressing, I serve this salad with my Lemon Vinaigrette (page 161), and a glass of Sangría (page 179).

SERVES 2

2 cups shredded iceberg lettuce

$^1/_2$ cup slivered almonds

1 medium papaya, seeded, peeled, and diced into 1-inch cubes

1 cup halved seedless green or red grapes

1 teaspoon chopped scallion, for garnish

$^1/_2$ cup Elsie's Lemon Vinaigrette (page 161)

1 Make a layer of lettuce and almond slivers in the bottom of a salad bowl.

2 Add the papaya cubes, followed by the grapes. Sprinkle the top with scallions. Drizzle the vinaigrette over the top and serve.

Ensalada de Zanahorias y Pasas   *Carrot and Raisin Salad*

Raisins are one of my favorite snacks; I love them with salted peanuts, in my *avena* (oatmeal), and of course in rice pudding. So basically, I like my *pasas* for breakfast, snacks, and desserts! Served with barbecued chicken or ribs, this is a wonderfully simple and refreshing summertime salad that Mami and I enjoy a lot. We especially like it chilled, right, Mami?

SERVES 4

One 16-ounce bag shredded carrots (or if you have the time, use 1 pound whole carrots and peel and shred them yourself)

$^1/_2$ cup dark raisins

1 teaspoon extra virgin olive oil

$^1/_2$ teaspoon sugar

$^1/_2$ teaspoon salt

Freshly ground black pepper

$^1/_2$ cup Hellmann's or Best Foods mayonnaise

In a large bowl, combine the carrots, raisins, olive oil, sugar, salt, and pepper to taste, and mix well. Add the mayonnaise and stir until well blended. Cover and refrigerate for at least an hour, or overnight.

Ensalada de Arroz *Rice Salad*

Rice salads are simple, inexpensive, and very versatile. I like them because they help me solve my left-over rice problem! But really, sometimes I make this salad simply because my family requests it. You can try using apple cider or white balsamic vinegar for a slightly different flavor, though my favorite is white vinegar. Serve with Garlic Bread (page 172) or Tostones (page 74).

SERVES 6

2 cups cooked Basic White Rice (page 171), made with 1^1/$_3$ cups chicken broth instead of water and ^{2}/$_3$ cup rice

2 cups drained canned or cooked frozen peas and carrots

^{1}/$_3$ cup plus 1 tablespoon extra virgin olive oil

1 medium yellow onion, peeled and chopped

1 medium green or red bell pepper, seeded and chopped

^{1}/$_3$ cup chopped fresh cilantro leaves

1 garlic clove, peeled and chopped

1^1/$_2$ tablespoons white vinegar

1 teaspoon salt

^{1}/$_4$ cup pimiento-stuffed Spanish green olives

1 Combine the rice and peas and carrots in a large bowl. Set aside.

2 Heat 1 tablespoon of the oil in a skillet over medium-high heat. Add the onion and pepper and cook, stirring frequently to prevent burning, until the onion is golden brown, about 8 minutes. Remove from the heat and let cool to room temperature.

3 Combine the cilantro, garlic, and vinegar in a blender or food processor. Add the remaining ^{1}/$_3$ cup of oil and the salt, blend to combine, and set aside.

4 Transfer the rice mixture to a large serving bowl or platter. Stir in the cooked onion and pepper. Pour the dressing over the salad and toss. Top with the olives and serve.

Melin's Potato Salad

Mi madre has prepared this potato salad every Thanksgiving as far back as I can remember. She can do it with her eyes closed! Many have tried to re-create this salad, but they weren't able to do it the way Mami did. One day I watched her and took notes; I couldn't believe how simple it was. Try to make this a day ahead of time so that the flavors meld together. Serve as a side dish any time, or even a lunch with Spicy Garlic String Beans (page 44).

SERVES 6 TO 8

5 pounds russet potatoes, unpeeled

Salt

1 red bell pepper, seeded and finely diced

1 green bell pepper, seeded and finely diced

1 large Spanish onion, peeled and finely diced

3 medium carrots, peeled and finely diced

One 32-ounce jar Hellmann's or Best Foods Mayonnaise
   (sorry, no exceptions here!)

1. Fill a stockpot with plenty of water. Wash the potatoes, but don't peel them (you'll see why) and add them to the stockpot. Bring to a boil, add salt, and cook until the potatoes are tender—or don't offer resistance when poked with a fork—15 to 20 minutes. Drain and set aside.

2. While the potatoes are still warm, use a butter knife to peel off the skin. (This is a trick Mami showed us for no-fuss, quick and easy peeling!)

3. When the potatoes are cool enough to handle, dice them into bite-size pieces and transfer to a large bowl. Add the peppers, onion, and carrots. Add 2 teaspoons salt and stir. Add the mayonnaise and stir well to coat. Serve immediately, or cover and refrigerate for up to 1 day to allow the flavors to meld.

Macaroni Salad with Shrimp

This sweet side salad with shrimp is so fantastic—and it transcends seasons and generations! Served chilled for summer barbecues or warm for Thanksgiving dinners, this versatile salad is sure to become a favorite with kids as well as adults.

SERVES 6

1 pound peeled and deveined medium shrimp, (thawed if frozen)

One 16-ounce box elbow macaroni

1 small onion, peeled and finely diced

3 garlic cloves, peeled and minced

$1/4$ cup sugar

$1/4$ cup extra virgin olive oil

One 16-ounce jar Hellmann's or Best Foods mayonnaise
   (sorry, no exceptions here!)

1 Bring a large stockpot filled about three-quarters of the way with water to a boil. Place the shrimp in the water and cook until they turn pink, about 5 minutes. Use a slotted spoon to remove them from the pot and drain on paper towels. Set aside in a large bowl.

2 Cook the macaroni according to the directions on the box, drain, and add to the shrimp. Stir in the onion, garlic, and sugar while the shrimp and pasta are still warm.

3 In a separate bowl, combine the oil and mayonnaise and mix well. Stir into the pasta and shrimp. Serve immediately, or cover and refrigerate for at least 1 hour or up to 2 days, and serve chilled.

Yuca con Cebolla   *Cassava with Sautéed Onions*

Cassava (or yuca) is the Puerto Rican spud. Don't let the barky outside fool you! The inside, once cooked, looks a bit like a potato, but has a unique delicate flavor that marries well with many dishes. Vegetarians like Ray's brother and sister-in-law enjoy cassava with eggs for breakfast, or this dish for lunch or dinner. I like to serve this as a side dish with pork chops or Pernil (page 134).

SERVES 4

2 pounds cassava (yuca)

Salt

2 teaspoons unsalted butter

2 large Vidalia onions, peeled and sliced into $1/4$-inch-thick rings

2 or 3 bay leaves

2 tablespoons white vinegar

Freshly ground black pepper

$1/4$ cup extra virgin olive oil

1 Fill a large stockpot with water and bring it to a slow boil.

2 Peel the thick cassava bark: Cut the pieces crosswise into 3-inch sections with a sharp knife. Stand a section upright on a cutting board. Starting at the top of the tuber, cut a strip of the bark and fibrous layer off with a downward motion of the knife. Rotate the cassava, and cut off the remaining bark in this manner. Repeat with the other sections.

3 Add the peeled cassava to the water, and raise the heat higher. When the water starts to fully boil, add salt. Cook the cassava 15 to 20 minutes, until tender—a knife or fork should go in without resistance.

4 Drain the cassava. Cut the pieces in half lengthwise, remove any fibrous strings from the center, and place the cassava in a casserole or baking dish.

5 Heat the butter in a medium skillet over low heat. Add the onions and bay leaves and stir. Add the vinegar along with some salt and pepper. Stir and cover. Cook, stirring occasionally, until onions are soft, about 8 minutes.

6 Remove from heat and pour on the top of the cassava. Drizzle the olive oil on top. Let the flavors meld for about 10 minutes before serving; the cassava should be slightly warm or at room temperature.

Surtido de Vegetales *Vegetable Medley—Beyond Broccoli*

Can you believe that there was a time when I couldn't see beyond broccoli? It's true. Despite the diverse cuisine I grew up with—which boasts a fusion of European, Afro-Caribbean, and Latin American cultures—my old standard veggie side was steamed broccoli, or sometimes broccoli with cheese. Luckily for my family and me, I decided to expand my horizons (after boring myself and wanting to explore), and I'm still discovering how many fabulous vegetables there are to enjoy in this world! This vegetable dish—sparked with a bit of *chorizo* (Latin-style sausage)—is pretty versatile, and very tasty. On nights when I'm just too tired to prepare a rice or pasta dish, I cook the preseasoned meat I keep in my freezer and serve it together with this dish—and everyone's happy!

SERVES 6

3 tablespoons unsalted butter

2 garlic cloves, peeled and crushed

1 large red bell pepper, seeded and coarsely chopped

1 large Vidalia onion, peeled and coarsely chopped

$1/_2$ cup finely diced chorizo (see Note)

3 medium zucchini, coarsely chopped

3 medium yellow summer squash, coarsely chopped

One 10-ounce package sliced mushrooms

Dash of red pepper flakes

Salt and freshly ground black pepper

1 In a large skillet over low heat, melt the butter. Add the garlic and cook until it's lightly browned, about 2 minutes.

2 Add the pepper, onion, and chorizo, stir to coat and continue cooking, stirring occasionally, until the pepper and onion begin to soften, about 10 minutes.

3 Add the zucchini, squash, and mushrooms. Continue cooking, stirring occasionally, until the squash softens, 7 to 10 minutes.

4 Add the pepper flakes (the hotter the better—for me, anyway!) and salt and pepper just before serving.

NOTE: Chorizo is available in Latin American groceries, as well as some larger supermarkets and butchers.

Spicy Garlic String Beans

Vegetables aren't usually a favorite of youngsters, and sometimes even we grown-ups don't eat enough. This dish came out of my attempt to eat more veggies; I decided if I'm going to enjoy them, I needed to spruce them up a bit. Ideally you'd use fresh beans here but let's face it: We're busy and sometimes don't have the time to deal with them! If you are using fresh beans, be sure to trim and rinse them before adding them to the pot. Serve this side dish with any dinner, or even by itself—with a leafy green salad (topped with Elsie's Lemon Vinaigrette, page 161) and crusty loaf of bread—for a light lunch.

SERVES 4 TO 6

1 teaspoon extra virgin olive oil

2 garlic cloves, peeled and minced

2 tablespoons unsalted butter

1 pound fresh or frozen whole string beans

Salt and freshly ground black pepper

Red pepper flakes

1 Heat the oil in a sauté pan over low heat. Add the garlic and cook, stirring, until it's lightly browned, about 2 minutes.

2 Add the butter and once it's melted, add the string beans. Stir to distribute the beans evenly in the pan, cover, and cook until they're slightly softened but still a bit crunchy, about 5 minutes for frozen beans, and a few minutes more for fresh.

3 Transfer the beans to a serving dish. Sprinkle salt, pepper, and pepper flakes on top and serve.

Stewed Okra

Okra, another one of Mami's favorites, is a vegetable that marries well with many others—like tomatoes, onions, corn, and peppers. Its delicate flavor is comparable to eggplant, but its texture is much different (and may seem very unusual to you if you've never tried it before). Popular in the South of the United States, okra is said to be originally from Africa, from whence it was brought to the Americas by slaves. Here, and throughout the Caribbean, Central, and South America, okra is found in many different dishes and in many forms, including raw, marinated, pickled, breaded, and fried. Look for young pods free of bruises; okra should be tender but not too soft, and not longer than 4 inches. I usually serve okra with Arroz con Gandules (page 95).

SERVES 4

2 teaspoons unsalted butter

1¹/₂ cups finely chopped onions

2 cups halved grape tomatoes

2 garlic cloves, peeled and chopped

2 teaspoons finely chopped fresh cilantro leaves

1¹/₂ pounds of fresh okra, washed and trimmed

Salt

Dash of freshly ground black pepper

1 In a 10-inch skillet, melt the butter over moderate heat. Add the onions and cook, stirring frequently, until softened, about 5 minutes.

2 Stir in the tomatoes, garlic, and cilantro and cook, stirring occasionally, until the tomatoes have softened, about 5 minutes.

3 Add the okra, salt to taste, and pepper, and cook until the okra is tender, about 15 minutes. Serve hot.

Elsie's Spiced-Up Corn

Corn on the cob is standard fare at our barbecues. After all, the kids love it! But one day, after getting tired of cleaning the corn out of my teeth, I decided I wanted to take care of the grown-ups too, and offer them an off-the-cob alternative—and that's how I came up with this colorful, sweet, and spicy delight. One suggestion: Make sure you cut close to the cob so that you get the whole kernel, as opposed to just part of it.

SERVES 4

6 to 8 ears corn on the cob

2 teaspoons extra virgin olive oil

$1/2$ teaspoon red pepper flakes

$1/2$ teaspoon chopped fresh cilantro leaves

Salt and freshly ground black pepper

1 Shuck the corn: Pull the outer husks down the ear to the base. Snap off the husks and stem. Use your hand to move any remaining silk (if it's stubborn, you can use a vegetable brush).

2 Stand the corn upright on its stem end on a cutting board or in a shallow dish. Cut the corn in a downward motion; cut close to release the kernels, but try not to cut the cob. Repeat while rotating the ear until all the kernels are removed.

3 Heat the oil in a large skillet over medium heat. Add the kernels, reduce the heat to low, and cook, stirring frequently, until the kernels are tender, 5 to 7 minutes; don't overcook the corn—the kernels should be tender but not mushy.

4 Sprinkle the corn with pepper flakes and mix well. Remove the corn from the heat and transfer to a serving bowl. Stir in the cilantro, season with salt and pepper to taste, and serve.

Guineos Sancochados *Boiled Green Bananas*

This side dish goes well with so many Puerto Rican meals. As in the case of plantains, *guineos* are vegetable-like in how we use them. And compared to some Latin American vegetables (like yautía and yuca), guineos are more commonly used by my relatives—probably because they're easier to peel! Though they're simple in flavor, they go beautifully with Bacalao Guisado (page 16), and of course, our traditional Pernil (page 134).

SERVES 4

1 bunch (4 to 6) green bananas

Salt

1 large Vidalia onion, peeled and sliced into $1/4$-inch rings

$1/4$ cup extra virgin olive oil

2 or 3 bay leaves

Freshly ground black pepper

1. Soak the bananas in warm water in a large bowl or in the sink for about 20 minutes; this will soften the skin and make peeling easier. Remove from the water, dry them, cut the ends off, and cut a slit lengthwise down the skin. Open the peel, using a knife or your hands, as if you were taking a jacket off somebody.

2. Fill a large stockpot three-quarters of the way with water and bring to a boil over high heat. Add the whole peeled bananas and a pinch of salt. Cook over high heat until the bananas are tender enough to stick a fork in without resistance, about 15 minutes. Drain them, and let them cool.

3. Place the onion rings in a large bowl. Add the olive oil, bay leaves, salt, and pepper and mix well. Slice the bananas in half lengthwise, if desired, and add to the bowl. Stir well to coat. Let marinate at room temperature for 10 minutes and remove bay leaves before serving.

Habichuelas Rosadas   *Red Beans*

Habichuelas rosadas are probably the most common of the beans made in Latin American restaurants. They are very versatile and unlike the red kidney beans that are larger and browner in color, or gandules, rosadas offer up just the right touch to white rice and any kind of meat. A bowl of rice, to me, is nothing without the beans to complement it. This bean dish is rich, thick, and full of flavor, and though I like it with white rice and ripe plantains, you can certainly eat it on its own right out of the pan! I recommend doubling the recipe and keeping it handy for later in the week.

SERVES 4

1 tablespoon extra virgin olive oil

$1/2$ cup canned tomato sauce

1 tablespoon Sofrito (page 158)

1 teaspoon Sazón (page 163)

1 cup peeled, diced calabaza (green or West Indian pumpkin; (see Note), cut into bite-size chunks

1 medium russet potato, peeled and diced into bite-size pieces

Two 15.5-ounce cans pink beans, drained

1 In a large saucepan over low heat, combine the olive oil, tomato sauce, sofrito, and sazón. Mix well, cover, and let cook until it starts to bubble, about 3 minutes.

2 Stir in the calabaza and potatoes. Cover and simmer until the potatoes just start to soften, about 5 minutes. Add the beans and $1^1/2$ cups water. Raise the heat to high, and cook uncovered, stirring occasionally, until the water starts to boil, about 3 minutes.

3 Reduce the heat to medium and cover. Cook until the calabaza and potatoes are very tender—even starting to dissolve—8 to 10 minutes. Serve immediately.

NOTE: Calabaza is available in Latin American and West Indian groceries, as well as some larger supermarkets.

Elsie's Turkey Tacos and Arroz con Pollo

Shrimp Ceviche

The traditional version of this South American–born fish dish is marinated in lime, lemon, or orange juice (and "cooked" by the acid of the citrus fruits) and then mixed with onions and chiles. This interpretation could be called a cousin of ceviche since the shrimp is already cooked! This simple yet elegant appetizer, which came to me via a Cuban connection, is especially gorgeous when served in a martini glass.

SERVES 6

1 pound peeled, deveined, and cooked large shrimp (thawed if frozen)

1 small tomato, seeded and finely chopped

$1/4$ cup finely chopped scallions, green parts only

Juice of $1/2$ a small lemon

2 tablespoons extra virgin olive oil

1 garlic clove, peeled and finely diced or crushed in a *pilón* or by a garlic press

1 tablespoon chopped fresh cilantro leaves

Salt and freshly ground black pepper

6 red lettuce leaves

6 lemon wedges

1 In a large bowl, combine the shrimp, tomato, scallions, lemon juice, and olive oil. Stir in the garlic, cilantro, and salt and pepper. Mix well. Cover and refrigerate for at least an hour.

2 When ready to serve, blanket six martini glasses with the lettuce leaves. Divide the shrimp mixture among the glasses, and serve with a wedge of lemon.

Escabeche de Pescado *Puerto Rican-Style Pickled Fish Fillets*

This style of fish can be found throughout the Caribbean, and also in Spain, France, Italy, and North Africa. Certain elements vary, but basically the fish is cooked—either poached or fried—and then marinated in a kind of vinegar or citrus sauce. Though some traditional recipes call for frying the whole fish, I find that using fillets makes it much easier—and kid friendly! Usually we make this ahead of time, let it marinate for a few hours or even overnight, and serve it cold. I discovered that it's also fabulous at room temperature.

SERVES 6

6 to 8 whiting or kingfish fillets (about 3 pounds)

Salt and freshly ground black pepper

All-purpose flour

One 16-ounce jar of roasted red peppers, liquid drained and reserved, sliced into thin strips

2 medium onions, peeled and sliced into thin rings

Half of an 7-ounce jar pimiento-stuffed Spanish green olives, drained

1 cup corn or vegetable oil, plus extra for frying

$1/4$ cup white vinegar

2 bay leaves

1 Place the fish fillets on a platter or on wax paper. Season on both sides with salt and pepper, and coat lightly with flour. Set aside.

2 In a bowl, combine the reserved roasted pepper liquid and pepper strips, onion rings, olives, 1 cup oil, and the vinegar and mix well. Stir in the bay leaves and set aside.

3 Pour about 2 inches of oil in a deep skillet set over high heat. Once the oil is very hot but not smoking, add the fillets without crowding the pan (you may have to fry them in batches). Cook each side until the fish are golden brown on both sides, about 8 minutes total. Remove and drain on a plate lined with paper towels.

4 Once the fillets are cooked and drained, place them in a deep baking dish. Pour the vinegar mixture over the fish; make sure it covers all of them. Let the fish sit for about 15 minutes before serving (if you want to serve them warm) or cover and refrigerate for at least 2 hours or overnight, and serve cold; remove bay leaves before serving.

Accidental Guacamole

My simple guacamole was created by accident. We were having fajitas one night, and I realized we didn't have any toppings. However, we did have a very ripe avocado. So I peeled and seeded the avocado, mashed it in my *pilón* (a traditional Puerto Rican bowl used as a vessel for mashing everything from garlic to coffee), and combined it with some additional flavors; the result was great. Now I make this very simple guacamole on purpose and serve it not only as a topping, but also as a side dish or appetizer with tostones or my favorite tortilla chips.

MAKES ABOUT ³/₄ CUP GUACAMOLE, ENOUGH TO TOP 6 FAJITAS

2 garlic cloves, peeled

Salt and freshly ground black pepper

1 large very ripe Hass avocado

$^1/_2$ lemon

1 Drop the garlic into a pilón or wooden bowl and mash it with a pestle. (If you don't have a pestle, use the back of a wooden spoon.) Add a dash of salt and pepper and mash together.

2 Cut the avocado in half lengthwise around the seed. Cup it between the palms of your hand and gently twist the halves apart. Use a knife to pry the pit out. Use a spoon to scoop out the avocado meat. Add the avocado to the pilón, a few pieces at a time, and continue mashing.

3 Cut the lemon half into quarters and squeeze a few drops of the juice into the mixture. Stir, taste for seasoning, adjust, and serve.

Media Noche *Cuban Sandwich*

Though this sandwich, in its original version, is from Cuba, it's also very popular in Puerto Rico and, of course, in New York. In Spanish we call it *media noche*, which means midnight—though this quick snack is a welcome treat any time. When my boys were younger, I often made these treats as an after-sports snack on weekdays and weekends.

MAKES 8 SANDWICHES

8 hotdog buns

Unsalted butter, softened

8 slices ($^1/_2$ pound) deli-sliced ham

8 slices ($^1/_2$ pound) deli-sliced Genoa salami

8 slices ($^1/_2$ pound) deli-sliced cheese (your choice)

1 Open the hot dog buns and spread each side with butter. Place one slice of ham, salami, and cheese on one side of each bun. Close the bun, and tuck in any of the meat or cheese pieces so they're not sticking out.

2 Melt a bit of butter in a large skillet over medium heat Place a few of the filled sandwiches in the skillet (you'll probably only be able to fit three or four at a time; do not overcrowd). Using a spatula, press to flatten each one. Cook until the bottom starts to brown, about 5 minutes.

3 Turn the sandwiches over, and toast the second sides until the cheese is melted and the bottoms are golden, about 5 minutes more.

4 Remove the sandwiches from the pan, slice diagonally, and serve.

Aguacates Rellenos *Stuffed Avocados*

When I unsuccessfully tried eliminating bread from my diet, I went back to my beloved avocado for help. Stuffed avocados are not uncommon in Puerto Rican cuisine; we use them as edible baskets (don't eat the skin, though!) for shrimp, crab—and one of my other favorites: tuna. So instead of eating my tuna salad as a sandwich between two slices of bread, I started stuffing it inside half of a pitted, unpeeled avocado. Well, as I said, my nonbread diet didn't work out too well... but this recipe is still one of my favorite lunches!

SERVES 2

One 6-ounce can tuna packed in water, drained

1 teaspoon finely chopped celery

1 teaspoon finely chopped onion

1 tablespoon Hellmann's or Best Foods mayonnaise

1 splash fresh lemon juice

Salt and freshly ground black pepper

1 small ripe Hass avocado, sliced in half and pitted

In a bowl, combine the tuna with the celery, onion, mayonnaise, and lemon juice. Add salt and pepper to taste. Spoon the tuna mixture into the avocado halves and serve.

Funche   *Puerto Rican Polenta*

Our older folks from Puerto Rico are not too keen on bacon and eggs for breakfast. *Avena* (oatmeal) was for the *trabajadores* (workers). But the comforting cornmeal flavor and texture of *funche* has won over a younger crowd—especially in my house! Popular since the Taínos lived on Puerto Rico, and reminiscent of the flavors of Guanimes (page 80), this farina-like treat is sure to win the hearts (and stomachs!) of older and younger fans in your home.

SERVES 4

1 cup fine yellow cornmeal

4 cups whole milk

2 or 3 cinnamon sticks or 1 teaspoon ground cinnamon

2 tablespoons unsalted butter

$^{1}/_{2}$ cup sugar

1 Sift the cornmeal through a strainer to make it even finer and set aside.

2 Heat the milk and cinnamon sticks in a large saucepan over low heat. Cook, stirring occasionally, until it starts to come to a soft boil, about 5 minutes. This will release the flavor of the cinnamon sticks into the milk. (Add the ground cinnamon after heating the milk, if you're not using the sticks.)

3 Add the butter and sugar, raise the heat to medium, and bring the mixture back to a low boil. Reduce the heat to low and, stirring continuously, slowly mix in the cornmeal. Cook, stirring constantly so the cornmeal doesn't lump or stick, until it becomes the consistency of grits or farina, about 5 minutes.

4 Remove the cinnamon sticks just before serving.

Tortilla de Papas con Queso *Spanish Omelet with Cheese*

It seemed liked dinners were so uncomplicated when the kids were young—mostly because they were much more flexible in their distinction between breakfast and dinner foods. (Believe it or not, I've even made oatmeal and pancakes for dinner!) This dish, my variation of the traditional *tortilla española*, is one I especially enjoy—for breakfast, lunch, or dinner. I make mine with the classic potatoes, but I've added the *toque puertoriqueño* (Puerto Rican touch) of adobo and cheese. Sometimes I top my omelet off with a sprinkle of cilantro or scallions. For dinner, I serve this with Garlic Bread (page 172), and a leafy green salad.

SERVES 6

2 tablespoons butter

1 small onion, peeled and chopped

3 medium russet potatoes, peeled and sliced into
   $1/8$-inch-thick rounds

6 large eggs

$1/2$ teaspoon Adobo (page 164)

$1/4$ cup shredded Cheddar cheese (about 1 ounce)

1 Melt the butter in a large skillet over low heat. Add the onion and cook, stirring, until the onions start to soften, about 5 minutes. Add the potatoes and cook, without stirring, until they start to brown on the bottom, about 5 minutes. Flip and cook without stirring until the potatoes are soft, about 7 minutes more.

2 In a bowl, combine the eggs and adobo and mix well. Pour the mixture on top of the onions and potatoes in the skillet, making sure it spreads out evenly and covers.

3 Check after a few minutes; when the eggs start to brown on the bottom, flip the omelet. (Note that this can be tricky! Some people use a plate to invert their omelets; I use a large spatula, or two standard size spatulas to turn the omelet over.) Cook on the second side until golden, about 3 minutes more.

4 Turn off the heat, sprinkle the cheese on top, and cover the skillet. Let the omelet sit for 5 minutes, until the cheese is melted. Cut into pie-shaped slices and serve.

Pimientos Rellenos *Stuffed Peppers*

Maybe part of the reason why I love this dish is because it brings me back to my childhood; when Mami used to make these, the sweet smell of roasted peppers would fill our home and we couldn't wait to taste the great combination of the soft rice, spiced meat, and toasted peppers. Here I've given you a recipe with white rice that works beautifully to capture the fresh flavors of the pepper and the seasoned meat. Pimientos Rellenos can be served as an appetizer or a lunch.

SERVES 6

6 large green bell peppers

4 cups (about 2 pounds) ground beef

1 tablespoon Adobo (page 164)

1 teaspoon Sazón (page 163)

4 cups Basic White Rice (page 171)

1 Preheat the oven to 350°F.

2 Cut a round hole in the top of each pepper and remove the stem and the seeds inside. Roast the peppers by placing them over a low to medium open gas flame on top of the stove, carefully turning them until they're evenly charred. Wrap them in foil or place them in a brown paper bag and let them sit until cool enough to handle (this will help make the peeling much easier). Use your fingers to peel off the charred skin.

3 Set the peppers stem-side up in a greased casserole (or cut off a thin layer off the bottom of the peppers to give them a flatter surface for balance and place them on a greased baking sheet.)

4 While the peppers are cooling, cook the ground beef in a large skillet over medium heat with the adobo and sazón, stirring frequently with a wooden spoon or using a potato masher to break up any large

Elsie's Turkey Tacos and Arroz con Pollo

chunks, until the meat is no longer pink, about 7 minutes. Remove from the heat, drain fat, and stir in the rice. Mix until well blended.

5 Using a tablespoon, gently scoop the meat and rice mixture into the peppers. Fill them almost to the top (not all the way, because it may expand slightly and you don't want it to spill out).

6 Bake until the peppers are tender, about 30 minutes. Serve immediately.

Fried Treats

Albondigas Rellenas *Stuffed Meatballs*

I'm not sure where the relationship between olives and ground beef started, but it's one that works well! Whether it's in a *picadillo* (spiced-up ground beef mixture) that's tucked into classic Argentine empanadas, or simply combined with pasta, the briny smooth olives balance the firm texture of the meat. I've always been a meatball fan so this quickly became one of my favorite cocktail party treats. I like to serve them on toothpicks with My Best Barbecue Sauce (page 168) for dipping.

MAKES 25 MEATBALLS

2 pounds lean ground beef

2 tablespoons Sofrito (page 158)

$1/4$ cup chopped fresh cilantro leaves

Extra virgin olive oil

$1/2$ cup seasoned bread crumbs

25 pimiento-stuffed Spanish green olives

Vegetable oil for frying

1. In a large bowl, combine the beef, sofrito, and cilantro. Use your hands or a wooden spoon to mix well.

2. Using your fingers, scoop up about 1 heaping tablespoonful of the meat mixture and flatten it in your palm. Place an olive in the middle and mold the meat to cover it, and using a circular motion, create a meatball. Repeat with the remaining meat mixture and olives.

3. Pour the breadcrumbs onto a flat plate. Roll each meatball in the breadcrumbs to evenly coat.

4. Fill a deep skillet with about 2 inches of oil and heat over high heat. Once the oil is hot but not smoking, start frying the meatballs in batches (without overcrowding). Cook until evenly browned, turning as needed, for about 7 minutes. Drain on paper towels, transfer to a platter with a side dish of toothpicks, and serve.

Bacalaítos   *Codfish Fritters*

Bacalaítos are just one of the many snacks that I grew up with. These codfish fritters, sold in stores called *cuchifritos* (which is also the name of another kind of appetizer-like treat sold in Puerto Rico, and of course in *El Barrio* in Manhattan, where I grew up) are served all year round. When I was a kid, as a special treat Mami would pick up a few fritters after school to hold us over until dinner was ready. Though I'm not sure what the secret was for our local store's bacalaítos, I've been making these very simple treats for years—and they've always been well received!

SERVES 5
(Makes about 10 fritters)

1 pound boneless dried codfish
2 cups all-purpose flour
Achiote Oil (page 162)
Vegetable oil for frying

1 Place the codfish in a large pot. Add enough water to cover it and let it soak for about 1 hour to remove some of the salt. After an hour, discard the water and refill with clean water. Bring the pot to a boil and cook until the fish is not too salty, about 10 minutes. (Taste a piece and you'll know right away if it's still too salty!) If it's fine, drain then rinse it and let it cool; otherwise give it another 10 minutes to soak, off the heat, before draining. When it's cool enough to handle, shred it into bite-size pieces using your fingers or a fork. Set it aside.

2 In a bowl, combine the flour and 1 cup water and add a tiny bit of achiote oil (which adds a bit of color). The consistency should be thin, like a watery pancake-like mixture. Stir in the codfish and mix well.

3 In a deep skillet or deep fryer, heat about three inches of oil over high heat; you want to be able to submerge the bacalaítos in the oil. When the oil is really hot but not smoking, use a ladle to pour the

batter into the oil to make pancakes 3 to 4 inches wide. They won't be in neat circles, but that's fine!

4 Fry the fritters until golden brown on both sides (you don't need to turn them because they're submerged in the oil), about 4 minutes. Drain on paper towels, and serve immediately.

Alcapurrias *Latin-Style Plantain and Meat Fritters*

This Puerto Rican treat, which is made differently by almost everyone, is a favorite in *El Barrio* (Spanish Harlem). When my kids were younger, they and their friends would always ask me to make these fritters, which I called Puerto Rican egg rolls because of their shape. Though it takes a bit of time to prepare them, it's certainly worth it! Serve these fritters with your favorite hot sauce.

SERVES 10 TO 15
(Makes about 20 fritters)

2 pounds lean ground beef

1 tablespoon Sofrito (page 158)

One 8-ounce can tomato sauce

$^1/_2$ cup whole pimiento-stuffed Spanish green olives, drained

Salt and freshly ground black pepper

8 green plantains

3 pounds green bananas

2 tablespoons Adobo (page 164)

2 tablespoons Achiote Oil (page 162)

Vegetable oil for frying

1 Prepare the stuffing: In a skillet, cook the ground beef over medium heat, stirring occasionally, until browned, about 10 minutes. Use a strainer or colander to drain the excess oil from the meat, and return the meat to the pan. Reduce the heat to low. Add the sofrito, tomato sauce, olives, salt, and pepper. Stir well, cover, and cook until the mixture starts to softly boil, 3 to 5 minutes. Turn off the heat and set the mixture aside.

2 Prepare the shell: Soak the plantains and green bananas in warm water in a large bowl or in the sink for about 20 minutes; this will soften the skin and make peeling easier. Remove them from the water, dry them, cut the ends off, and cut a slit lengthwise down the skin. Open and remove the peel, using a knife or your hands, as if you were taking a jacket off somebody.

3 Using a grater, grate the bananas and plantains. The resulting mixture will texturally resemble cooked oatmeal. Add the adobo and the achiote oil, which will both soften and color the bananas. Use a fork to smooth the mixture. If it's still too lumpy or coarse you can run it through a blender or process with a hand mixer; it should be smooth.

4 Spread a piece of clear wrap or wax paper on a flat surface. Take about 3 tablespoons of the banana mixture and place it on the wrap. Using the back of a spoon, flatten it and spread it out evenly. It should be about 6 inches wide, the size of a small tortilla. Now take 2 tablespoons of the meat mixture (don't forget an olive!) and place it on top of the flattened banana paste. Using the ends of the wrap, fold over first one side to cover the meat mixture, and then the other. (The wrap helps to use your hand without touching the dough.) Fold up the ends into a kind of egg-roll shape. Try to wrap up the meat without letting it show or stick out. Repeat with the remaining dough and filling.

5 Heat about 2 inches of oil in a deep skillet over high heat; the oil should be deep enough to submerge several fritters at a time. As soon as the oil is very hot but not smoking, carefully add the fritters, one at a time and without crowding them. Fry until golden brown, about 8 minutes total, and, using tongs, remove them to drain on paper towels. Serve immediately.

Plátanos Rellenos *Stuffed Plantains*

Plátanos rellenos are great because they combine two of my favorite things: sweet plantains and *carne molida a la criolla* (ground beef seasoned our Puerto Rican way!). Here you mash the plantains into a kind of dough that's stuffed with the delicious sofrito and sazón-flavored ground beef. The trick for making this delectable treat is to keep the meat moist (which the sofrito helps with) and using ripe—but not too ripe—plantains.

SERVES 4 TO 6

4 to 6 ripe plantains (yellow with minimal black spots)

1¹/₂ pounds lean ground beef

1 tablespoon Sofrito (page 158)

1 tablespoon Sazón (page 163)

1 cup fine yellow cornmeal

Vegetable oil for frying

1 Fill a large stockpot with water and bring to a boil.

2 Peel the plantains: Cut off the ends and cut a slit lengthwise down the middle (don't make the cut deeper than the skin). Open and remove the peel, using a knife or your hands, as if you were taking a jacket off somebody. Cut the plantains crosswise into quarters.

3 In a skillet over medium heat, combine the ground beef with the sofrito and sazón. Cook, stirring frequently, until the ground beef is browned and the mixture starts to bubble, 10 to 12 minutes. Remove from the heat and let cool.

4 Once the water starts to boil, add the plantains to the stockpot. Stir once and let them cook over medium high heat until tender, about 12 minutes. (They don't have to be too soft because they're going to be further cooked in the skillet!) Drain the plantains.

5 Pour the cornmeal into a flat plate.

6 Once the plantains are cool enough to handle, use a potato masher to mash the plantains into a kind of dough that you'll stuff with the meat mixture. Make a small pancake of mashed plantains in your hand. Scoop up a tablespoonful of the meat mixture, fold it inside, and roll it into a small baseball-size ball. Make sure the meat is not sticking out. Repeat with the remaining plantain and meat mixtures. Roll each of the balls in the cornmeal and set aside.

7 Fill a deep skillet with about 2 inches of oil and heat over high heat. As soon as the oil is very hot but not smoking, fry the balls in batches (don't overcrowd them) until they're golden brown, about 10 minutes. Drain on paper towels and serve immediately.

Beef Empanadas

Of course Mami made her empanadas by preparing her own dough, which you have the option of doing. I find if I don't use the convenient frozen turnover dough, I just won't make these delicious savory pastries! My kids and their friends have always loved empanadas. In fact when all my boys were younger, they requested that I make these for their birthday parties (and I served them instead of potato chips). The beauty of the empanada is not only that it's *deliciosa*, but also that it can be stuffed with just about anything; Nicholas likes the ones with just cheese; Mark and Eric like theirs with ground beef and cheese. I like mine with ground beef and red pepper flakes. I've even stuffed them with shredded leftover chicken cutlets! Serve these at kids' parties with punch or soda, or at adult parties with a salad and Piña Coladas (page 178) or Sangría (page 179).

MAKES 10 EMPANADAS

1 pound ground beef

$1/2$ cup canned tomato sauce

1 teaspoon Sofrito (page 158)

Salt and freshly ground black pepper

10 frozen turnover dough discs, thawed and separated

8 ounces (about 2 cups) shredded mozzarella cheese

Vegetable oil for frying

Hot sauce (optional)

1 In a skillet over medium heat, combine the ground beef, tomato sauce, sofrito, and salt and pepper to taste. Let simmer, stirring frequently, until the ground beef is cooked, about 10 minutes. Set aside.

2 Place the turnover disks on a work surface and roll them out individually so that the dough stretches just a bit (this thins them out and makes them easier to work with).

3 Spoon about a tablespoon of the meat mixture into the middle of each turnover. Sprinkle some mozzarella cheese on top. Fold over one side of the dough to form a half-moon shape. Tuck in any meat or cheese that may stick out. Using the tines of a fork, press down on the rim of the half moon (not the folded side) to seal the edges together. Repeat until you've filled all the turnovers.

4 Pour about 2 inches of vegetable oil into a heavy skillet, and heat over high heat. When the oil is really hot but not smoking, gently add the turnovers without crowding (you'll have to cook them in batches). Fry on each side until golden brown, about 3 minutes per side. You'll know when they're done because they turn golden brown and puff up in the middle. Drain on paper towels and serve hot, with hot sauce if desired.

Relleno de Papa   *Beef-Stuffed Potatoes*

These treats sit proudly against the windows of the famous Cuchifritos on 116th Street in East Harlem. This popular potato appetizer can be made with fresh Idaho or russet potatoes, but I've made them in no time using instant mashed potatoes! If you have time, do use the real potatoes, but if you don't, try my easier version. If you want to make a complete meal, simply serve them with rice and beans and a leafy green salad and you'll be set.

MAKES 6 TO 8 PIECES

One 12-ounce can corned beef

$^1/_2$ cup canned tomato sauce

1 teaspoon Sofrito (page 158)

1 teaspoon Sazón (page 163)

6 to 8 russet potatoes, peeled, boiled, and mashed, or instant mashed potatoes for 6 servings

1 cup all-purpose flour

1 cup fine yellow cornmeal

Vegetable oil for frying

1 Empty the corned beef into a medium skillet. Stir in $^1/_2$ cup water, the tomato sauce, sofrito, and sazón. Cover and cook over medium heat, stirring occasionally, until it starts to bubble, about 10 minutes. Set aside.

2 Divide the potatoes into 6 to 8 portions. Make a small pancake with one portion of the mashed potatoes in your hand. Scoop up about 1 tablespoonful of the meat mixture, and fold it inside. Roll it into a small baseball-size ball. Make sure the meat is not sticking out. Repeat with the remaining potato and meat mixture.

3 Pour the flour and cornmeal on flat plates. Roll each of the stuffed balls in the flour first, and then in the cornmeal.

4 Fill a deep skillet with about 4 inches of oil and heat over high heat. Fry the balls in batches (don't overcrowd them) until golden brown, about 10 minutes. Drain on paper towels and serve immediately.

Chicharrón de Pollo de Elsie *Elsie's Fried Chicken*

Chicharrón, which means fried-up crispy, is one of Ray's favorites (in fact if I don't make it for a long time, he buys it at one of our local Latin restaurants!). Though traditionally this dish is made with all parts of the chicken, I prefer to use my kids' favorite parts: the breast and the thighs. Serve this as a side dish or appetizer, or as a whole meal with rice and beans, and a salad, with my Mojito (page 159).

SERVES 4

2 pounds chicken breast with the bone or thighs, cut into bite-size pieces

1 tablespoon Adobo (page 164)

2 cups vegetable oil

1. In a large bowl, combine the chicken pieces with the adobo; I use my hands to make sure the pieces are well coated.

1. Heat the oil in a skillet over high heat. As soon as it's very hot but not smoking, add the chicken pieces (without overcrowding). Fry in batches until golden brown, about 8 minutes total. Drain on paper towels and serve immediately.

Plátanos Dulces *Fried Sweet Plantains*

Sweet plantains have saved so many meals for me! Whenever I want to "fill" the plate, in true Puerto Rican custom, I fry up a couple of these and add them on. (Nico's favorite breakfast is still fried eggs with the yolk broken, served next to my fried sweet plantains.) The nice thing about this side dish—aside from the fact that it's so easy to prepare and very tasty—is that it goes with breakfast, lunch, and dinner.

SERVES 4

4 very ripe plantains (almost black)

$^1/_4$ cup vegetable oil

1 Prepare the plantains: Cut the ends off and cut a slit lengthwise down the middle. Open and remove the peel, using a knife or your hands, as if you were taking a jacket off somebody. Cut the plantains, either diagonally or in straight round slices, into 1-inch-thick pieces.

1 Heat the oil in a large skillet over medium heat. Fry the plantains until golden brown, about 3 minutes on each side. Drain on paper towels and serve.

Tostones *Fried Green Plantains*

Every Puerto Rican—and Dominican—knows how wonderful these twice-fried green plantain chips are! Making these snacks in my house was always a joint effort: One of my sisters would fry them, the other would squash them, and I would make the mojito—or sauce. Serve these as a side dish or snack with Mojito (page 159), and your favorite cocktails or cold drinks.

SERVES 8 TO 10

4 to 6 green plantains
Vegetable oil for frying

1 Prepare the plantains: Soak them in warm water in a large bowl or in the sink for about 20 minutes; this will soften the skin and make peeling easier. Remove the plantains from the water, dry them, cut the ends off, and then cut a slit lengthwise down the skin. Open the peel, using a knife or your hands, as if you were taking a jacket off somebody. Cut the plantains diagonally into 2-inch-thick slices (you're going to be smashing them, so they'll get thinner).

2 In a deep skillet, heat about 2 inches of oil over high heat. Add the plantain pieces, without overloading the pan. (You may have to fry them in batches.) Fry until they're light brown on both sides, 3 to 5 minutes total. Remove and drain them on paper towels. Reserve the oil; you're going to use it again.

3 Line the bottom of a sheet pan or any work surface with aluminum foil. Take each piece of fried plantain and, using a spatula or something heavy, smash each one so that it spreads to form a round shape (they're usually a bit uneven).

4 Reheat the oil and fry the flattened pieces, without crowding, until they're a bit darker brown and crispy, just about 2 minutes. Remove and drain on paper towels. Serve immediately.

Arañitas   *Crispy Plantain Treats*

My friend Madeline, who moved to Brooklyn after a lifetime in Puerto Rico, taught me how to make this typical and delicious snack. Once you see these adorable crispy creations you'll understand why they're called "little spiders" in Spanish! Tasty and delicious, and of course similar in flavor to Tostones (page 74), these are great on their own with Mojito Rojo (page 160), or sprinkled on top of soups and salads.

SERVES 4

4 green plantains
1 teaspoon Adobo (page 164)
Vegetable oil for frying

1. Prepare the plantains: Soak them in warm water in a large bowl or in the sink for about 20 minutes; this will soften the skin and make peeling easier. Remove the plantains from the water, dry them, cut the ends off, and cut a slit lengthwise down the skin. Open and remove the peel, using a knife or your hands, as if you were taking a jacket off somebody. Grate them, using the large holes on a box grater (these uneven grated pieces are what create the spider look).

2. Season the grated plantain with the adobo and mix well with a spoon. Using your hand, scoop up about 1 tablespoon of the grated plantain and flatten slightly. Repeat with the remaining plantain.

3. Fill a deep skillet with about 2 inches of oil and heat over high heat. Fry the plantain patties in the hot oil until golden brown, turning once to make sure it cooks evenly (about 3 minutes on each side). Drain on paper towels and serve.

Guineitos Fritos   *Fried Dwarf Bananas*

Anybody who's lived or traveled to the Caribbean knows that we love bananas. (Actually, bananas are the number one fruit in the United States!) I grew up with bananas prepared in so many ways: fried, boiled, pureed, and of course, eaten fresh. This dish, made with the smaller and very sweet dwarf or finger bananas, is quite versatile. I first served it to my boys along with rice and black beans and they loved it. But you could also serve these bananas as a dessert, topped with ice cream.

SERVES 6

8 to 10 ripe dwarf or finger bananas (about 2 pounds)

Vegetable oil for frying

2 cups all-purpose flour

1 teaspoon Sazón (page 163)

1. Peel the bananas and set aside.

2. Fill a deep skillet with about 2 inches of oil and heat over medium heat; you want to be able to submerge the bananas (whole) in the hot oil.

3. Meanwhile, pour the flour and $2^1/_2$ cups water into a large bowl. Using a whisk or hand mixer, combine to make a batter. Add the sazón. The batter should not be too thick; if it is, add a little more water.

4. Dip the bananas in, one at a time, and transfer to the hot oil in batches to avoid overcrowding. Fry until golden, 6 to 8 minutes Drain on paper towels and serve immediately.

Arepas de Maíz *Corn Fritters*

I grew up with this delicious finger food, which is similar to the *rellenos* (stuffed treats) in this book, but much simpler because the main ingredients are cornmeal and your favorite cheese! Recently Mami and I visited with my Tía Lydia during an early afternoon and she prepared some arepas for us. Tía had yellow cheese, so she used that. Within minutes, we were sitting together, snacking and talking! My mom and aunt began reminiscing how my *abuelita* would prepare them for my *abuelo* as an afternoon snack.

SERVES 4 TO 6
(makes 5 to 7 arepas)

2 cups fine yellow cornmeal

1 teaspoon salt

1 tablespoon sugar

1 cup thickly shredded Cheddar or mozzarella cheese
  (about 4 ounces)

Vegetable oil for frying

1. Pour the cornmeal into a bowl and set aside.

2. Meanwhile, in a small saucepan, bring 1 cup water to a low boil. Add the salt and sugar and stir until they dissolve. Remove the water from the heat, and pour it into the bowl with the cornmeal, stirring constantly. The texture of the mixture should be soft, but solid enough to mold.

3. When the dough is cool enough to handle, scoop up about a third of a cup of dough. Use a smaller spoon or your fingers to flatten it, and create a small pocket in the middle. In that recess, add about 1 teaspoon of cheese. Using your hands, cover the cheese with the dough, and roll into a slightly-flattened pancake shape about 4 inches in diameter. Repeat with the remaining dough and cheese.

4. Fill a deep skillet with about 4 inches of oil and heat over high heat. Fry the fritters in batches, without overcrowding, until golden, about 8 minutes. Drain on paper towels and serve immediately.

Batatas Dulces   *Sweet Potatoes with Marshmallows*

Boiled, baked, or fried, the sweet potato or yam is a popular part of Puerto Rican cuisine. It's used both as a side vegetable, as well as a *postre* (dessert) when making a regional sweet-potato cake. Mami frequently cooked *batatas* when we were little, but it was my sister Mary who brought this more American version of the marshmallow-blanketed side dish into our family's Thanksgiving menu. I've used it as a side dish to many meat entrées (great with roast pork!). Mary—and our kids—just love our batatas super *dulces* (very sweet), but you can always lighten up on the syrup.

SERVES 6

2 pounds sweet potatoes, peeled and cut into 1-inch-thick slices

$1/4$ pound (1 stick) unsalted butter, melted

$1/2$ cup maple syrup

$1/2$ cup dark brown sugar

1 tablespoon ground cinnamon

1 tablespoon ground nutmeg

Half a 10.5-ounce bag miniature marshmallows

1 Preheat the oven to 350°F.

2 In a shallow medium baking pan, arrange the sweet potatoes in layers. Pour the melted butter on top, followed by the syrup. Sprinkle with the sugar, cinnamon, and nutmeg. Top with an even layer of marshmallows.

3 Bake until the sweet potatoes are tender and nicely glazed by the marshmallows, about 30 minutes. Serve immediately.

Yuca Frita *Yuca Fries*

One of my favorite fast foods in the world is French fries, but yuca fries are a wonderful—and sometimes preferred—second. Great served as appetizers or as a side dish with pork or other meat, these treats will quickly win you over. Though you can certainly use fresh yuca, here I'm suggesting frozen which is much simpler—and faster—to deal with. I serve these to guests and family on a large platter with a dish of my Mojito (page 159) for dipping.

MAKES ABOUT 25 FRIES

One 24-ounce bag frozen yuca (cassava)

Salt

Vegetable oil for frying

1 Fill a stockpot with water and raise the heat to high. Once the water starts to boil, add the frozen yuca and 2 teaspoons salt. Cook until the yuca is tender yet still firm (you don't want to overcook it or it will break apart), about 20 minutes. Drain the yuca and set it aside to cool.

2 When the yuca is cool enough to handle, cut the pieces in half and remove the stringy part in the center. Cut the yuca into sticks about 2 inches long and $1/2$ inch wide.

3 Preheat the oven to 200°F.

4 Fill a deep skillet with about 2 inches of oil and heat over high heat until the oil reaches a temperature of 375°F, or until a piece of yuca sizzles when placed in the oil. Add a few yuca pieces at a time to avoid overcrowding (and so the oil temperature doesn't go down). Fry the yuca until golden on all sides, 5 to 7 minutes, turning gently with a slotted spoon. Drain on a paper towels and keep warm in a 200°F oven until you've finished frying all of the yuca. Serve hot.

Guanimes de Maíz *Puerto Rican Tamales*

Tamales have a long history in the Americas. Though they vary from country to country, they're essentially cornmeal cakes, stuffed with a sweet or savory filling, wrapped in plant leaves or corn husks, and steamed until firm. In this case, I'm using parchment paper—because I usually have that on hand. Though they take some time to prepare, these tamales are worth every moment! *Guanimes* can be great for breakfast with eggs, and wonderful for dinner with Guisado de Berenjena y Bacalao (page 18).

MAKES 6 TAMALES

1 cup fine yellow cornmeal

1 cup sugar

1 teaspoon plus 1 pinch salt

$^1/_2$ teaspoon ground cinnamon

1 cup whole milk

Parchment paper and cooking string

1 In a large bowl, combine the cornmeal, sugar, salt, and cinnamon. Stir in the milk, and mix well until it comes together to form a dough.

2 Cut the parchment paper into six 8-inch squares. Put 2 tablespoons of the mixture into the center of a parchment paper square, spread it out with the spoon so that it's about 5 inches long and 2 inches wide. Fold up the sides and ends and tie the package closed with cooking string. Repeat until all of the corn mixture has been used.

3 Fill a large stockpot about three-quarters of the way with water and bring to a boil. Add a pinch of salt. Place the wrapped guanimes into the boiling water, reduce the heat to medium, and cook until firm, about 40 minutes. Remove from the pot to a plate and carefully cut the strings. Unwrap the guanimes and serve.

Bolitas de Queso *Cheese Balls*

Anyone who knows me knows that there are certain foods that I just go crazy for; cheese is one of them! Not only do I like cheese on its own, I also like putting it in just about everything. These cheese balls are the perfect appetizer for me: They're simple, quick, and incredibly tasty. On Sunday afternoons, I often like to visit with friends and family (stragglers from the big Saturday dinners I usually cook!), sit back with Ray, sip sangría, and eat those addictive treats.

MAKES ABOUT 12 BOLITAS

$1/2$ pound shredded Gouda or Cheddar cheese (about 2 cups)

2 large eggs

2 tablespoons cornstarch

1 cup plain dry bread crumbs

Vegetable oil for frying

1 In a medium bowl, stir together the cheese, eggs, and cornstarch to form a dough.

2 Pour the breadcrumbs onto a flat surface or a plate.

3 Take about 1 tablespoon of the cheese mixture and use your hands to roll it into a small ball, about the size of a meatball. Repeat with the remaining dough. Coat the cheese balls by rolling them individually in the bread crumbs, and set aside.

4 Heat a large skillet with enough vegetable oil to submerge the balls (about 1 inch deep). When the oil is hot but not smoking, add the balls to the skillet without crowding, and cook until golden, about 5 minutes. (You may have to fry them in batches.) Drain on paper towels, and serve right away.

Main Dishes Made with Rice

Even people who don't speak Spanish can understand this name of one of our most popular dishes: *Arroz con Pollo*. Just as pasta is for so many Italian meals, rice is a key component in Puerto Rican dishes. Like pasta, rice blends with numerous and varied flavors; you can add just about anything to it. (Also, it's economical!)

I've included my top rice dishes here, but I must tell you that my experimentation with this fundamental ingredient is ongoing. I hope you'll enjoy these dishes, find your favorites, and perhaps create your own variations!

Carne al Estilo Irlandés con Arroz

Rice with Corned Beef

Mom's corned beef night was always an indicator that all the "real" meat was gone from the fridge, and that she hadn't made it back to the market yet. This very simple dish with cured beef—which most people have in their pantry—is made extra delicious with one of my family's favorites: Plátanos Dulces (page 73).

SERVES 4 TO 6

Two 15-ounce cans corned beef hash

$^1/_2$ cup canned tomato sauce

1 teaspoon Sofrito (page 158)

1 teaspoon Sazón (page 163)

2 cups frozen corn kernels, thawed, or one 15.25-ounce can, drained

2 cups Basic White Rice (page 171)

$^1/_2$ recipe Plátanos Dulces (page 73; use 2 plantains)

1 Empty the corned beef hash into a medium skillet. Stir in $^1/_2$ cup water, the tomato sauce, sofrito, and sazón. Cover and cook over medium heat, stirring occasionally, until it starts to bubble, about 8 minutes.

2 Add the corn, mix well, and cook until heated through and the meat is still moist but not too wet, about 5 minutes. Serve immediately over white rice, topped with the plátanos dulces.

Arroz con Salchicha *Rice with Sausage*

You've probably seen those cans of Vienna sausages on supermarket shelves and passed them right by. Well, now I urge you to try these small hot dogs—Puerto Rican style! This recipe is so tasty, and so very simple! I serve it with a side dish of Plátanos Dulces (page 73), and a leafy green salad topped with fresh avocado slices.

SERVES 4

$^1/_4$ cup vegetable oil

One 8-ounce can tomato sauce

2 tablespoons Achiote Oil (page 162) or

1 teaspoon Sazón (page 163)

1 tablespoon Sofrito (page 158)

One 9-ounce can Vienna sausages

2 cups long-grain white rice, rinsed

Salt

1 In a medium *caldero* or heavy pot, heat the oil over medium heat. Add the tomato sauce, achiote oil, and sofrito and stir well. Cover and cook the sauce over low heat until it begins to simmer, about 10 minutes.

2 Slice the Vienna sausages into $^1/_4$-inch-thick round pieces, add them to the pot, and stir well. Cover and simmer until heated through, about 5 minutes.

3 Add the rice and stir to coat well with the sausage mixture. Stir in 4 cups water and increase the heat to high. Cook uncovered, stirring frequently until the rice is moist and the water is mostly evaporated, 5 to 10 minutes.

4 Reduce the heat to low, cover, and cook until the rice is fluffy, about 15 minutes more. Serve immediately.

Arroz con Costillas *Rice with Ribs*

I'm a great lover of one-pot meals, and this is one of my kids' favorites. The boys love this dish because they're huge sparerib fans, and I love it because I was tired of spending so much time cooking spareribs, and found that the boneless version offered me a tasty and time-saving alternative. Served with corn on the side (Elsie's Spiced-Up Corn, page 46, or Mexican-Style Corn, page 169), and a nice leafy green salad, this is certainly a simple work-night meal!

SERVES 4

2 pounds boneless spareribs, cut into 2-inch pieces

2 tablespoons Sofrito (page 158)

2 teaspoons Sazón (page 163)

²/₃ cup vegetable oil

One 8-ounce can tomato sauce

2 cups long-grain white rice, rinsed

2 teaspoons salt

1 In a large *caldero* or heavy pot, combine the spareribs with the sofrito and sazón, stirring to coat. Turn on the heat to medium and cover the pot. Cook, stirring occasionally, until the meat has browned slightly, about 25 minutes. Add the oil and tomato sauce, cover, and cook until the sauce starts to boil, about 3 minutes.

2 Stir in the rice and mix well. Raise the heat to high and mix in 4 cups water. Add the salt. Cook uncovered until the water starts to evaporate, about 5 minutes.

3 Reduce the heat to low, cover the pot, and cook until the rice is nice and fluffy, 18 to 20 minutes.

Arroz con Pollo *Rice with Chicken*

From the Puerto Ricans on down to the Argentines, just about every Latin American has their own recipe for chicken with rice. My family loves our sofrito and sazón-flavored version. Served with salad or with Spicy Garlic String Beans (page 44), this is a great meal for weekday evenings, or longer weekend meals.

SERVES 6

2¹/₂ pounds chicken pieces (1 whole chicken, cut up, or a combination of drumsticks and thighs)

2 tablespoons Sofrito (page 158)

1 teaspoon Sazón (page 163)

One 8-ounce can tomato sauce

¹/₄ cup vegetable oil

2 cups long-grain white rice, rinsed

Salt

1. Place the chicken pieces in a large *caldero* or heavy pot. Add the sofrito and sazón and mix together with a big spoon to coat the chicken. Cover and cook over medium heat, stirring from time to time to prevent sticking (you don't need to add water because the steam creates a broth), until the meat is no longer pink, 15 to 20 minutes.

2. Mix in the tomato sauce and oil. Cover and cook until bubbling, another 10 minutes.

3. Add the rice and mix well. Add 4 cups water while stirring, so the rice doesn't stick. Raise the heat to high and cook uncovered until the water has almost evaporated but the rice still seems moist, about 10 minutes.

4. Reduce the heat to low, cover, and cook until the rice is nice and fluffy, 10 to 15 minutes more. Serve immediately.

Elsie's Seafood Paella

In my family, I am the seafood paella master! Because my home has become party headquarters for most occasions (and actually most Saturday nights!), and because I love to vary my dishes, I've found that paella is perfect to serve: It's flexible, always tasty, and very pretty. This is my basic recipe for a crowd, but you can add or remove ingredients depending on your and your families' favorites.

SERVES 6 TO 8

1 head garlic, separated into cloves and peeled

2 cups (4 sticks) unsalted butter

3 or 4 lobster tails, about 1 pound each

1^1/$_2$ dozen littleneck clams, scrubbed clean

^{1}/$_4$ cup vegetable oil

2 tablespoons Sofrito (page 158)

^{1}/$_2$ cup Achiote Oil (page 162)

3 chorizo links (about 8 ounces), cut into bite-size pieces (see Note)

One 10-ounce can chopped or minced baby clams, drained

^{1}/$_2$ cup Spanish green olives (with pits), drained

4 cups canned chicken broth

2^1/$_2$ cups long-grain white rice, rinsed

Salt and freshly ground black pepper

2 pounds bay scallops (thawed if frozen)

2 pounds peeled and deveined medium shrimp (thawed if frozen)

1 Preheat the oven to 325°F.

2 Drop the garlic into a *pilón* or wooden bowl about 2 to 3 inches wide, and mash it with a pestle. (If you don't have a pestle, use the back of a wooden spoon.)

3 Melt the butter in small saucepan, stir in the mashed garlic, and set aside. Give the lobster tails a quick rinse under cold water. Lay them flat, meat side up, on a baking sheet. Drizzle some of the melted garlic butter on top, saving some to drizzle on the clams. Bake in the oven until the shells turn red, 10 to 12 minutes. Set aside.

4 Place the littleneck clams on a baking sheet and bake until all the clams open, 10 to 12 minutes. (Throw out the ones that don't open.) Drizzle the remaining garlic butter over the clams and set aside. In a large *caldero* or heavy pot, add the vegetable oil, sofrito, and achiote oil and let simmer over low heat. Add the chorizo to the pot. Cook, stirring occasionally, until lightly browned, about 5 minutes. Add the canned clams and olives and stir.

5 Stir in the chicken broth and raise the heat to high. Once it starts to boil, add the rice and mix well. Sprinkle with salt and pepper, and cook until the broth has slightly evaporated, but is still visible.

6 Add the scallops and shrimp. Cover and cook over low heat until the rice is cooked, about 15 minutes.

7 Spoon the rice into a large bowl or serving platter. Lay the garlic-buttered lobster tails and clams on top of the rice and serve.

NOTE: Chorizo is available in Latin American groceries, as well as some larger supermarkets and butchers.

Arroz con Bacalao *Rice with Codfish*

The season of Lent has always been observed in my home. In keeping with that tradition of no-meat Fridays, I had to get creative in order not to blow my weekly food budget on expensive fish for my family. This dish was one of the results of my creativity! Like my Seafood Paella (page 88), the flavors of the fish and the rice—along with the *criolla* seasonings—meld together to make a delicious meal. For a light dinner, serve with my Pickled Cabbage (page 170); for heartier fare, serve with your favorite beans.

SERVES 6

1¹/₂ pounds boneless dried codfish

²/₃ cup vegetable oil

One 7-to-8-ounce jar roasted pimientos, diced into bite-size chunks (save the liquid)

One 8-ounce can tomato sauce

2 tablespoons Sofrito (page 158)

1 teaspoon Sazón (page 163)

2 cups long-grain white rice, rinsed

1. Place the codfish in a large pot. Add enough water to cover it and let it soak for about 1 hour to remove some of the salt. After an hour, discard the water and refill with clean water. Bring the pot to a boil and cook until the fish is not too salty, about 10 minutes. (Taste a piece and you'll know right away if it's still too salty!) If it's fine, drain it and let it cool; otherwise give it another 10 minutes to soak, off the heat, before draining. When it's cool enough to handle, shred it into bite-size pieces using your fingers or a fork. Set it aside.

2. Heat the oil in a medium *caldero* or heavy pot over medium heat. Add the pimientos and their liquid, the tomato sauce, sofrito, and sazón. Stir well to combine. Cover and simmer until it starts to boil,

about 5 minutes. Uncover, add the shredded codfish, and stir. Cover and let simmer over low heat until heated through, about 5 minutes.

3 Add the rice and stir it well to coat. Increase the heat to high and add 4 cups water. Continue cooking over high heat until the water is no longer visible, about 5 minutes.

4 Reduce the heat to low, cover the pot, and cook the rice until is tender but not dry, 18 to 20 minutes. Serve immediately.

Arroz Negro con Calamari   *Black Rice with Calamari*

The first time I tried this dish I was a little hesitant because I had never seen black rice before. The rice, which is colored by the ink of the calamari, not only has interesting visual tones, but also great taste. The exotic presentation of this dish, along with the flavors, are both enhanced by the fact that it's very easy to prepare. Serve this rice alone, with beans, or ideally with Tostones (page 74).

SERVES 6

$^1/_4$ cup vegetable oil

Two 4-to- 6-ounce cans squid in its own ink (*calamares en su tinta*)

1 tablespoon Sofrito (page 158)

2 cups long-grain white rice, rinsed

$^1/_4$ cup pimiento-stuffed Spanish green olives, drained

Salt and freshly ground black pepper

1 In a medium *caldero* or heavy pot, heat the oil over medium heat. Stir in the calamari with its ink and sofrito and cook, stirring frequently, until it starts to simmer, about 5 minutes.

2 Add the rice and olives and mix well. Stir in 4 cups water, salt, and pepper (I like a lot of pepper with this!). Raise the heat to medium-high, bring the water to a boil, reduce the heat to medium, and let simmer until the water becomes partly evaporated, about 10 minutes.

3 Reduce the heat to low, cover the pot, and cook until the rice is still tender but not dry, 18 to 20 minutes. Serve immediately.

Arroz con Maíz *Rice with Corn*

Arroz con maíz is my favorite rice dish of all—and luckily for me my boys feel the same way! My sister Linda (whose boys crave corn so much that they'd even eat it in pancakes) also makes this dish for her crowd. There's something about the taste of the sweet corn together with the sazón that makes it irresistible to my family—and hopefully to yours, too!

SERVES 4

$1/2$ cup canned tomato sauce

2 tablespoons vegetable oil

1 tablespoon Sofrito (page 158)

2 cups frozen sweet corn kernels, or one 15.25-ounce can, drained

1 tablespoon Sazón (page 163)

2 cups long-grain white rice, rinsed

2 teaspoons salt

1 In a medium *caldero* or heavy pot, combine the tomato sauce, oil, and sofrito. Stir well and bring to a boil over medium heat. Stir in the corn and sazón and mix well. Let cook until it starts to softly boil, about 3 minutes.

2 Add the rice and stir to coat. Add 4 cups water, stir again, and raise the heat to high. Stir in the salt.

3 When the water starts to evaporate, after about 5 minutes, cover the pot and reduce the heat to low. Cook until the rice is nice and fluffy, 18 to 20 minutes. Serve warm.

Arroz un Poquito Picante con Vegetales

Slightly Spicy Vegetable Rice

I'm always looking for new ways to marry my favorite staple, rice, with other flavors I enjoy. In this dish, the sofrito, paprika, black pepper, and chorizo offer just enough spark to perk up the rice. This rice is perfect as a main dish, but you might want to serve it as a side dish with grilled fish or chicken.

SERVES 6

$^1/_4$ cup vegetable oil

2 chorizo links (4 to 5 ounces), diced into small pieces (see Note)

$^1/_2$ cup My Meaty Spaghetti Sauce (page 166), or your favorite tomato sauce

2 tablespoons Sofrito (page 158)

2 cups long-grain white rice, rinsed

1 tablespoon paprika

1 teaspoon salt

1 cup frozen peas and carrots, thawed

One 7-ounce can corn, drained or $^3/_4$ cup frozen corn

Freshly ground black pepper

1 Heat the oil in a medium *caldero* or heavy pot over low heat. Add the chorizo and cook until the chorizo starts to brown, about 5 minutes. Stir in the tomato sauce and sofrito and cook until it starts to bubble, about 3 minutes.

2 Add the rice and 4 cups water, and stir well to combine. Stir in the paprika and salt. Cover and let cook over high heat until the water starts to evaporate, about 5 minutes.

3 Stir in the peas and carrots and corn. Add pepper (the more the better!). Cover, reduce the heat to low, and continue cooking until rice is nice and fluffy, 18 to 20 minutes. Serve immediately.

NOTE: Chorizo is available in Latin American groceries, as well as some larger supermarkets and butchers.

Elsie's Turkey Tacos and Arroz con Pollo

Arroz con Gandules   *Rice with Pigeon Peas*

It wasn't until I was a bit older that I realized that this tasty dish was representative of my culture! *Arroz con gandules* may be Puerto Rico's most popular dish. Though every family has its own recipe, this is an adaptation of the one I grew up with. Of course my mom, when she was younger, back in Puerto Rico, used to use fresh beans; in New York she bought dried peas and soaked them overnight to make this, but with our crazy schedules, I needed to make changes to make it simpler and without sacrificing the integrity of the flavors. As long as I've got my sofrito in the fridge, I can whip this up within thirty minutes.

SERVES 6

2 tablespoons vegetable oil

One 15- to 16-ounce can pigeon peas (*gandules*), drained

$^1/_2$ cup pimiento-stuffed Spanish green olives, drained

One 8-ounce can tomato sauce

1 teaspoon Sazón (page 163)

$^1/_2$ pound cooked ham, diced into $^1/_4$- to $^1/_2$-inch cubes

1 tablespoon Sofrito (page 158)

2 cups long-grain white rice, rinsed

Salt

1 Heat the oil in a medium *caldero* or heavy pot over medium heat. Stir in the peas, olives, tomato sauce, and sazón and bring to a simmer. Stir in the ham and sofrito and let simmer until heated through, 2 to 3 minutes.

2 Stir in the rice, and mix until it is well coated with the sauce. Add 4 cups water and raise the heat. Once the mixture has come to a boil, add salt, reduce the heat to low, and cover.

3 Cook until most of the water is evaporated but the rice is nice and fluffy (the rice shouldn't dry out), 10 to 12 minutes. Add salt and serve warm.

Arroz con Frijoles Negros   *Rice with Black Beans*

Of all the rice dishes I have, except—of course—my paella, this is the prettiest. The combination of colors, not to mention the flavors, is fantastic. The first time I had rice with black beans was years ago in one of my favorite Dominican restaurants in the Bronx. Though I loved the contrast of black and white, I felt it needed more color, so I added one of my favorites: roasted peppers. The thinly sliced pepper strips, laid over the black and white backdrop, which is drizzled with the pepper juice, make this dish perfect! Serve with a side dish of Plátanos Dulces (page 73) and a green salad.

SERVES 6

1/4 cup vegetable oil

1/2 cup canned tomato sauce

2 tablespoons Sofrito (page 158)

1 teaspoon Sazón (page 163)

One 7- to- 8-ounce jar roasted red peppers

One 15.5-ounce can black beans, drained

2 cups long-grain white rice, rinsed

Salt and freshly ground black pepper

1 In a medium *caldero* or heavy pot, heat the oil over medium heat. Add the tomato sauce, sofrito, and sazón and stir well. Cook until the sauce begins to simmer, about 5 minutes.

2 Meanwhile, remove the roasted peppers from the jar over the pot, letting the juice drip into the tomato sauce mixture. Slice the peppers into thin pieces, about 1 inch long, and set aside. Save a few for garnish and add the rest to the pot, along with the beans, and mix well.

3 Add the rice and stir to coat well with the tomato and bean mixture. Stir in 4 cups water and increase the heat to high. Cook, stirring frequently, until the rice is moist and the water is mostly evaporated, 7 to 10 minutes.

4 Reduce the heat to low, cover, and cook until the rice is tender but not dry, 18 to 20 minutes. Add salt and pepper to taste, and garnish with the remaining sliced peppers before serving.

Arroz con Habichuelas Rosadas   *Rice with Red Beans*

Preparation of this very traditional rice dish is a breeze; I can whip this up in no time. My rice with red beans may be simple, but it has depth. It can certainly be served on its own (or with my favorite Spiced-Up Corn, page 46, on the side), or as a side dish with your favorite meat. I like leaving the cilantro sprigs in as an extra visual touch (of course, I love the flavor, too!) but you can take them out if you'd like. Though I make this on the day I'm serving it, this rice dish tastes even better the next day.

SERVES 6

¹/₄ cup vegetable oil

¹/₂ cup canned tomato sauce

2 tablespoon Sofrito (page 158)

1 teaspoon Sazón (page 163)

One 15.5-ounce can pink beans, drained

¹/₄ cup *alcaparrado* (a mixture of olives and capers; see Note)

2 or 3 sprigs fresh cilantro, including the leaves

2 cups long-grain white rice, rinsed

Salt and freshly ground black pepper

1 In a medium *caldero* or heavy pot, combine the oil, tomato sauce, sofrito, and sazón and cook over low heat until the sauce starts to softly boil, about 5 minutes. Add the beans, alcaparrado, and cilantro and mix well. Cover and continue cooking until the cilantro looks wilted, about 5 minutes.

2 Add the rice and stir it for about 2 minutes to coat well. Add 4 cups water, and raise the heat to high. Sprinkle in some salt and pepper and adjust as you like (I like mine with more pepper than salt!).

3 Continue to cook over high heat until you can no longer see the water, about 5 minutes.

4 Cover and reduce the heat to low. Cook until the rice is nice and fluffy, 18 to 20 minutes. Serve immediately.

NOTE: Alcaparrado is available in Latin American groceries, as well as some larger supermarkets.

Arroz con Garbanzos   *Rice with Chickpeas*

The buttery, nutlike flavor of garbanzos goes with so many dishes. I've always loved chickpeas in salads, but wanted to create a rice dish with them. Because they're soft in flavor, I decided to marry them with a bit of seasoning, so I added the salty and tasty flavors of *salchichón* (hard salami) and caper-stuffed olives. This colorful rice dish certainly doesn't require any additional salt. Serve with a side of salad or Tostones (page 74).

SERVES 6

$^1/_2$ cup vegetable oil

One 8-ounce can tomato sauce

1 cup diced salchichón or hard salami

1 teaspoon Sazón (page 163)

2 tablespoons Sofrito (page 158)

$^1/_2$ cup Spanish green olives stuffed with capers (see Note)

One 15- to 16-ounce can garbanzo beans (chickpeas), drained

2 cups long-grain white rice, rinsed

1 In a medium *caldero* or heavy pot, heat the oil over medium heat. Stir in the tomato sauce, salami, sazón, and sofrito and stir well. Cover and simmer until the sauce starts to boil, about 3 minutes.

2 Add the olives and beans. Cover again and let simmer until heated through, about 5 minutes. Stir in the rice and mix well to coat. Add 4 cups water and raise the heat to high. Cook uncovered until the water is no longer visible, about 5 minutes.

3 Reduce the heat to low, cover the pot, and cook until the rice is nice and fluffy, 18 to 20 minutes.

NOTE: Caper-stuffed olives are available in Latin American groceries, as well as some larger supermarkets.

Poultry, Meat, and Other Main Dishes

Now we come to the most important dishes of them all: the main dishes or *platos principales*. These are, after all, the main attraction! In this section you'll enjoy an array of colorful and delicious dishes, most of which can be put together in practically no time at all.

Growing up in a large family taught me a lot about cooking for a crowd. Now that I have my own large family, my main dishes are what I'm most proud of. This collection is a combination of what I learned over the years from Mami and *mis tías* (my aunts) as well as my own creations (now tried and true!) that I developed to feed my hungry boys. I hope you and your family will soon find your own favorites—and not only expand your main dish repertoire, but also create variations based on your family's favorite flavors. Enjoy!

Turkey Tacos

Anybody who has teenage boys knows that it's not easy to get them to hang out with the old parents! But I swear that taco night with the boys was like board game night at my place—it really got us all together in one room at the same time. In fact, it was the only time I could get them interested in helping. All I had to say was, "The quicker everything's diced, the quicker we'll eat!" You never saw three boys move so fast. Since that very first night we enjoyed them together, it's become a tradition that we all look forward to.

SERVES 4 TO 6

2 pounds ground turkey or beef

1 teaspoon Sazón (page 163)

Salt and freshly ground black pepper

$^1/_2$ cup canned tomato sauce

12 corn tortillas

Vegetable oil

FIXINGS

1 medium tomato, finely chopped

1 medium onion, peeled and finely chopped

$^1/_2$ head iceberg lettuce, thinly shredded

$^1/_2$ cup finely chopped fresh cilantro leaves

8 ounces (2 cups) shredded Cheddar cheese

Tabasco sauce (optional)

1 In a large skillet over medium heat, add the turkey meat and Sazón, and season with salt and pepper. Cook, stirring occasionally with a wooden spoon or using a potato masher to break up the meat, until well done, about 10 minutes. Use a strainer or colander to drain the excess oil from the meat, and return the meat to the pan. Add the tomato sauce and simmer to heat through, 2 to 3 minutes. Remove the pan from the heat and let cool.

2 Meanwhile, heat a large skillet with a small amount of vegetable oil (just enough to coat the pan). Once heated, add about 3 tortillas (or fewer if you have a small skillet) so that they sit alongside each other without overlapping too much.

3 Spoon some of the meat mixture right on top of each tortilla. (Don't let the meat spill over or it will splatter and can burn you.) Using a fork or spatula, fold the tortillas in half to form a half-moon shapes with the meat in the middle and press down. When lightly browned on one side, about 5 minutes, flip them over to cook the other side. Cook until that side is browned as well, about 5 minutes more.

4 Set cooked tortillas on a large platter lined with paper towels to allow for the excess oil to drain. Repeat the process with the remaining tortillas.

5 Serve from a platter (without paper towels!) with fixings nearby for everyone to add as they please.

Elsie's Turkey Chili on Baked Potatoes

I created my chili recipe when Ray and I decided it was time to diet. However, the big issue with us was the portion size. So though the chili really isn't fattening, you're not supposed to eat too much of it—and Ray and I, thinking we were actually losing weight (!!), couldn't help eating almost the whole pot. Well, the diet didn't stick, but we all enjoyed the recipe so much that we've kept it. Of course, you can make the chili on its own, but we especially enjoy it stuffed into baked potatoes, and topped with shredded cheese. This and a salad make a great dinner. Besides, you can always make the chili ahead of time, and simply bake the potatoes on the night you're serving these treats.

SERVES 6

FOR THE CHILI

1 pound ground turkey

2 garlic cloves, peeled and minced

1 small red or green bell pepper, seeded and finely diced

1 small onion, peeled and diced

1 medium zucchini, cut into bite-size pieces

1 medium yellow squash, cut into bite-size pieces

One 28-ounce can crushed tomatoes

Red pepper flakes (optional)

Salt and freshly ground black pepper

6 large russet potatoes, cleaned but not peeled

Extra virgin olive oil for drizzling

$3/4$ to 1 cup shredded mozzarella or Cheddar cheese (3 to 4 ounces)

1 First prepare the chili: In a large skillet, cook the turkey meat over low heat, stirring to break it up, until it starts to brown, about 5 minutes.

2 Add the garlic and mix well. Stir in the bell pepper and onion. Cover and simmer, stirring occasionally, until they start to soften, about 5 minutes.

3 Add the zucchini and squash and stir well. Stir in the crushed tomatoes and pepper flakes. (I suggest starting with a small amount, and after it cooks a bit, adding more according to taste.) Cover and cook on low until the vegetables are tender, about 15 minutes. Add salt and pepper to taste, and perhaps more pepper flakes!

4 Preheat the oven to 325°F.

5 Prepare the potatoes: Cut the potatoes in half lengthwise and place them on a baking sheet, skin side down. Drizzle about 2 teaspoons of oil over the top of each one. Bake the potatoes until they're tender (so that you can poke a fork in with no resistance), about 30 minutes.

6 Scoop about $1/4$ cup of chili on top of each potato half. Top with about a tablespoon of shredded cheese (or more, as desired). Return the potatoes to the oven, and bake until the cheese has melted, about 10 minutes. Serve immediately.

Chicken Fajitas

Maybe it's the fact that each person makes it the way he or she wants it, but this meal is inspiring. All my boys would perk up after their long days at school or work to make these festive dinnertime treats. The toppings for my chicken fajitas are optional, but I like putting them all on! Set the fixings out in colorful individual bowls with serving utensils.

SERVES 4 TO 6

2 or 3 chicken breasts with bones (about 2 pounds)

2 tablespoons extra virgin olive oil

1 large red bell pepper, seeded and sliced into thin 1-inch-long strips

1 large green bell pepper, seeded and sliced into thin 1-inch-long strips

1 large onion, peeled and sliced into thin 1-inch-long strips

$1/2$ cup canned tomato sauce

1 teaspoon Sazón (page 163)

Salt and freshly ground black pepper

10 corn tortillas

FIXINGS

$1/4$ cup jarred sliced jalapeño peppers

2 cups shredded Cheddar or mozzarella cheese (about 8 ounces)

2 cups My Favorite Salsa (page 165), or your favorite salsa

1 cup Accidental Guacamole (page 52)

1 cup sour cream

One 15- to 16-ounce can refried beans (Nicholas's favorite!), heated

Tabasco sauce

1. Fill a stockpot three-quarters of the way with water and bring to a boil. Add the chicken and cook until it is no longer pink, about 20 minutes. Drain and allow the chicken to cool for about 10 minutes.

2. Meanwhile, heat the oil in a large skillet over medium heat. Add the sliced peppers and onion and stir to coat with the oil. Cover and cook, stirring occasionally, until the vegetables have softened, about 10 minutes. Remove from the heat and set aside.

3. Once the chicken is cool enough to handle, remove the skin and shred the meat with a fork in a downward motion. Discard the bones and add the meat to the peppers and onions.

4. Stir the tomato sauce into the chicken mixture in the skillet. Add sazón and salt and pepper. Cook over medium heat, stirring frequently, until the mixture starts to simmer, about 5 minutes.

5. Just before the chicken mixture is ready, place your corn tortillas, wrapped in a paper towel, on a plate and microwave just to warm the tortillas, about 1 minute.

6. To serve, spoon (or let guests spoon) some of the chicken mixture into the middle of each tortilla. Have guests choose their own fixings, roll up their tortillas, and enjoy!

Tasty Turkey Wings

Roles in my house are very clear on Thanksgiving: Ray does the turkey and lasagna, and I make everything else. (This has been the way we've done it for years and years!) One year Ray—who is a big fan of this holiday—decided that we needed to do something about the great demand for turkey wings. After all, he felt that since everyone wanted the wings, and since the bird only came with two, he should accommodate them by making an extra batch. His solution has certainly created a new and welcome Thanksgiving tradition in our home. Ray's delicious and previously top-secret marinade is sure to win new fans any time of year! Make the marinade ahead of time so that you can let the wings sit in it overnight.

SERVES 6

$2/3$ cup white vinegar

$2/3$ cup extra virgin olive oil

6 garlic cloves, peeled and minced

3 tablespoons Adobo (page 164)

1 teaspoon Sazón (page 163)

Salt and freshly ground black pepper

6 to 8 turkey wings

1 In a large bowl, whisk together the vinegar, olive oil, garlic, adobo, sazón, and salt and pepper. Add the turkey wings and stir; make sure they're well coated. Cover and refrigerate for at least an hour, or ideally overnight.

2 Preheat the oven to 325°F.

3 Place the marinated turkey wings in a large roasting pan and bake, covered, until they're cooked (if you can poke a fork into the wing and you can easily pull a piece of meat from it, it's done), about 1 hour. Serve hot or at room temperature.

Mexican-Style Chicken Cutlets

I've always loved Mexican food, but I especially enjoy the flavor touches that a good guacamole or excellent salsa can add to many dishes. This thinking was what led me to the creation of this dish. I'll never forget Nicholas's first words upon seeing dinner that evening: "What *is* this?" Though he was initially put off by what he perceived as chaos on his plate, after one bite, he was smitten! Since that time, I make this easy and now highly requested dinner regularly. I usually serve this with Arroz con Maíz (page 93).

SERVES 6

2¹/₂ pounds boneless chicken cutlets

Salt and freshly ground black pepper

2 tablespoons vegetable oil

16 ounces (4 cups) shredded Cheddar cheese

2 cups My Favorite Salsa (page 165), or your favorite salsa

¹/₄ cup chopped fresh cilantro leaves

1 cup sour cream (optional)

1. Preheat the oven to 375°F.

2. Season the cutlets with salt and pepper. Heat the oil in a large skillet over medium heat and add the cutlets. Cook just until browned, about 3 minutes on each side.

3. Transfer the cutlets to a baking dish. Bake for 10 minutes, then top each one with a small handful of evenly sprinkled cheese. Continue baking until the chicken is cooked through, and the cheese is melted, about 15 minutes.

4. Transfer the cutlets to serving plates, drizzle salsa on top of each cutlet, sprinkle with the cilantro, add a dollop of sour cream (if desired), and serve.

Pollo Estofado   *Stuffed Chicken*

If there is one thing I know for sure, it's that Latinos need lots of flavor in their dishes! Like many other *puertoriqueños*, I depend on my sofrito and sazón to add the tasty touches I crave. But roast chicken—another one of my favorites—inspires me to be more creative with my seasoning techniques. Here I've chosen three ingredients I'm not only crazy about, but that I always have on hand: bacon, garlic, and butter. Served with Basic White Rice (page 171), and a leafy green salad, this makes a wonderful fall or winter dinner.

SERVES 4 TO 6

One 3-pound chicken, giblets removed, rinsed, and patted dry

6 strips bacon

Kitchen string

4 tablespoons unsalted butter, cut into 4 to 6 thin squares

3 garlic cloves, peeled and crushed

2 teaspoons salt

2 teaspoons freshly ground black pepper

1 Preheat the oven to 325°F.

2 Place the chicken breast side up in a roasting pan. Take one of the bacon strips and roll it tightly. Repeat with the remaining pieces, and stuff them into the cavity of the chicken. Use the kitchen string to tightly tie the legs of the chicken together.

3 Using the dull side of a butter knife, gently separate the skin above the breast, trying not to break it. With the butter knife, place the butter squares between the skin and the meat; this butter will melt and add both moisture and flavor to the white meat. Use the butter knife to spread the crushed garlic between the skin and the meat. (Don't worry about the underside of the bird; that will be flavored by the drippings, and also that meat is the most flavorful.)

4 Season the entire chicken with salt and pepper. Cover with a lid or aluminum foil and place in the oven. After 20 minutes, uncover and baste the chicken with the liquid on the bottom of the pan. Cover again, and bake until the chicken is almost cooked (no longer pink; the skin on the leg, when punctured with a fork or knife, should not release a red liquid), about 10 minutes.

5 Uncover and bake until golden and cooked through, about 10 minutes more. Let rest for a few minutes before serving.

Baked Barbecue Chicken

I'm not really big on baked or poached meats, but I do enjoy crispy fried chicken or anything with a chewy skin—and I love the sweet flavor of barbecue sauce. This dish offers you a healthier alternative to frying, and it's much easier because you can put it in the oven, and get busy doing other things. Serve this chicken with Arroz con Maíz (page 93).

SERVES 6 TO 8

8 to 10 skin-on, bone-in chicken thighs (about $2^1/_2$ pounds)

1 tablespoon Adobo (page 164)

1 tablespoon extra virgin olive oil

$^1/_2$ cup My Best Barbecue Sauce (page 168), your favorite jarred barbecue sauce, or honey

1 Preheat the oven to 350°F.

2 In a large bowl, season the chicken thighs with the adobo, and toss to coat. Arrange the chicken thighs skin side up, flat alongside each other in a rectangular baking dish. Drizzle with olive oil and place in the oven.

3 Bake until the chicken is no longer pink and it becomes as crispy as you like it, 30 to 45 minutes; the chicken will start to sizzle because of the oil you drizzled, along with its own natural juices.

4 Brush on the barbecue sauce and bake until cooked through and golden, about 10 minutes more. Serve immediately or at room temperature.

Ropa Vieja de Pollo *Pulled Chicken*

Ropa vieja, which literally means old clothes, is originally from Cuba. The meat is cooked, then shredded like rags (and sometimes cooked again). In this version, I use chicken, seasoned with sazón and roasted red peppers—along with the sweet and sour flavors of ketchup and vinegar. Simple yet so tasty, this chicken goes perfectly well with Basic White Rice (page 171) and Elsie's Spiced-Up Corn (page 46).

SERVES 4

4 boneless chicken cutlets (about 1½ pounds)

2 tablespoons ketchup

2 tablespoons extra virgin olive oil

2 teaspoons white vinegar

1 teaspoon Sazón (page 163)

One 16-ounce jar roasted red peppers, drained and sliced thin

1 large onion, peeled and sliced into thin rings

1. Fill a stockpot three-quarters of the way with water and bring to a boil. Add the chicken cutlets, and cook until they're no longer pink, about 10 minutes. Drain and set aside.

2. In a medium bowl, combine the ketchup, oil, vinegar, and sazón. Add the pimientos and onion and stir to combine.

3. When the chicken is cool enough to handle, using a fork or your fingers, thinly shred it. Add it to the mixture in the bowl, stir together so that the chicken is well coated, and serve.

Pollo con Crema de Cilantro *Creamy Chicken with Cilantro*

I've always been a huge fan of creamy, cheesy Alfredo sauce; I love the balance of the soft cream and the salty cheese flavors. Inspired by that, I decided to come up with something that balances with cream, but that incorporates something more Latino: the flavors of cilantro and sazón. This *Alfredo al Latino* chicken should be served on top of your favorite pasta, Basic White Rice (page 171), or Tostones (page 74).

SERVES 6

4 tablespoons ($^1/_2$ stick) unsalted butter

6 boneless chicken breasts (about 3 pounds)

Salt and freshly ground black pepper

2 cups (about 2 bunches) coarsely chopped fresh cilantro leaves

$^1/_2$ cup heavy cream

1 chicken bouillon cube

1 teaspoon Sazón (page 163)

1 Melt the butter in a large skillet over medium heat. Add the chicken breasts, sprinkle with salt and pepper, cover, and cook, turning at least once, until the chicken is no longer pink, about 20 minutes.

2 Meanwhile, in a blender, combine the cilantro, 1 cup water, the cream, bouillon cube, and sazón. Process until well blended.

3 Uncover the chicken, add the cream mixture to the skillet, and simmer over low heat, stirring occasionally, until the chicken is tender, about 10 minutes. Serve immediately.

Pollo al Ajillo   *Garlic Roasted Chicken*

Who doesn't love garlic? In my family, we've always been garlic aficionados. My brother is probably its biggest fan; he swears it cures anything. (In fact, he once gave my brother-in-law a drink of garlic water when he was feeling a bit under the weather!) I like the subtle and deep flavor garlic adds to many dishes. In fact, when I make my sofrito, I put more garlic in than any of the other ingredients. This chicken dish is great with Basic White Rice (171), with some extra garlic-wine sauce drizzled over the top.

SERVES 4

$1/_2$ cup extra virgin olive oil

One 3-pound whole chicken, cut up, or 3 pounds chicken drumsticks and thighs

1 teaspoon Sazón (page 163)

8 to 10 garlic cloves, peeled and diced

1 cup chardonnay, or other dry white wine

1 pinch each of salt and freshly ground black pepper

1. Heat the oil in a large skillet over medium heat. Add the chicken pieces. Cook the chicken, turning once, until it's golden on both sides, about 18 minutes total.

2. Sprinkle the sazón on top of the chicken pieces. Add the garlic and continue cooking, uncovered, until the garlic starts to soften, about 2 minutes.

3. Slowly pour the wine over the chicken. Cover and cook until the chicken is cooked through and tender, about 15 minutes. Add salt and pepper and serve immediately.

Pechugas à la Fricasé *Chicken Fricassee*

Variations of this classic chicken dish are quite popular in Puerto Rico. Though the name, which is said to come from the French *frire* (to fry) and *casser* (to break) shows its European roots, this is clearly the Puerto Rican version. When Ray's mom Mercedes first made this for me, I was amazed that it was so easy. Basically she just put everything together, and baked it up! Serve with Spicy Garlic String Beans (page 44).

SERVES 4

4 split chicken breasts on the bone
   (about ³/₄ pound each, 3 pounds total)

¹/₄ cup white vinegar

3 tablespoons extra virgin olive oil

2 tablespoons Adobo (page 164)

1 teaspoon Sazón (page 163)

3 garlic cloves, peeled and diced

1 large onion, peeled and sliced into thin rings

Salt and freshly ground black pepper

1 Preheat the oven to 300°F.

2 Place the chicken in a single layer in a baking pan, bone side down. Combine the vinegar, oil, adobo, and sazón in a bowl and mix well before pouring on top of the chicken—make sure the pieces are evenly coated). Sprinkle the garlic on top. Loosely cover with a sheet of aluminum foil.

3 Bake until the chicken is no longer pink, about 45 minutes.

4 Remove the foil, add the onion slices, and bake until they're tender, about 10 minutes. Add salt and pepper to taste just before serving.

Sausage and Penne Pasta with Elsie's Vinaigrette

I'd always been a big fan of the combination of oil, vinegar, garlic, and lemon juice, and often wondered where else—aside from topping salads—I could use my vinaigrette as a flavor enhancer. One evening, I had my chance. Friends had stopped by for an impromptu summertime visit, and we invited them to stay for dinner. Forced to whip up something quickly and without too much fuss, I perused my kitchen and found a box of penne pasta in the cupboard, along with some sausage and my vinaigrette dressing in the fridge. I quickly went to work and before too long, a new favorite was born! This now highly requested dish can be served warm or chilled, but always with crusty Garlic Bread (page 172).

SERVES 6

3 links hot Italian sausage (about $1/2$ pound)

3 links sweet Italian sausage (about $1/2$ pound)

One 16-ounce box penne pasta

1 cup Elsie's Lemon Vinaigrette (page 161),
   or your favorite Italian dressing

Freshly grated Parmesan cheese

1. Bring a large pot of water to a boil.

2. Cut a lengthwise slit down all the sausage links and peel off the casings. Heat a large skillet over medium heat. Add the sausage and cook, stirring frequently with a wooden spoon or using a potato masher to break up the larger chunks of meat, until the sausage meat is cooked through and no longer pink, about 20 minutes. Drain the sausage of excess liquid.

3. Meanwhile, cook the pasta in the boiling water according to the directions on the box.

4. Drain the pasta and pour it into a large bowl. Immediately pour in the dressing, followed by the cooked sausage, and mix well. Serve immediately, or cover and chill for at least 2 hours, or up to 6. Serve at room temperature, or microwave to heat. Sprinkle Parmesan cheese to taste on top just before serving.

Pastelón de Plátano *Puerto Rican Lasagna*

This delicious and hearty dish, called *Pastelón de Plátano* both in Puerto Rico and in the Dominican Republic, is similar to its Italian cousin, only instead of noodles we use our Caribbean plantains! My lasagna is perfect as a main course, served over Basic White Rice (page 171) with a salad and Garlic Bread (page 172), or even as a side dish.

SERVES 4 TO 6

2 tablespoons extra virgin olive oil

1 medium onion, peeled and finely diced

2 garlic cloves, peeled and diced

2 pounds lean ground beef

One 14.5-ounce can diced tomatoes

1 tablespoon tomato paste

2 teaspoons Sazón (page 163)

¹/₄ teaspoon salt

¹/₄ teaspoon freshly ground black pepper

1 pinch dried oregano

6 to 8 very ripe plantains (almost black)

16 ounces (4 cups) shredded mozzarella cheese

¹/₄ cup chopped fresh parsley

1 Heat the oil in a large skillet over medium heat. Add the onion and garlic, and cook, stirring occasionally, until the onions are transparent and the garlic is golden, about 5 minutes.

2 Add the ground beef and cook, stirring frequently, until it's no longer pink and the liquid has evaporated, 10 to 12 minutes.

3 Add the tomatoes, tomato paste, sazón, salt, pepper, and oregano and stir well. Reduce the heat to low and let simmer, stirring occasionally, until the mixture bubbles, about 5 minutes.

4 Preheat the oven to 325°F.

5 Prepare the plantains: Cut the ends off and cut a slit lengthwise down the middle. Open and remove the peel, using a knife or your hands, as if you were taking a jacket off somebody. Halve them lengthwise.

6 In a 9 by 13-inch baking pan, ladle enough sauce to line the bottom. Place a single layer of plantains on top. Add more sauce on top, and evenly sprinkle a layer of mozzarella on top of the sauce. Continue repeating layers until the ingredients are used up, but finish with a layer of mozzarella. Sprinkle the parsley on top.

7 Bake, covered with aluminum foil, until the cheese starts to melt, about 30 minutes.

8 Remove the cover and continue baking until the top is golden brown, about 10 minutes. Remove from the oven and let rest for about 10 minutes. Cut into squares, and serve.

Elsie's Baked Ziti

I'm not sure when they started calling me "The Queen of Baked Ziti," but baked ziti was my signature dish for years! In fact, before I started expanding my culinary repertoire, I made it for every holiday celebration—just as we would make *Pernil* (roast pork shoulder, page 134) What I like about this dish is that it is not only well loved, but also very easy to prepare—and simple to double (and even triple) for larger crowds. Serve hot, with plenty of Garlic Bread (page 172) and a leafy green salad.

SERVES 8 TO 10

1½ boxes (16 ounces each) ziti or penne

1 pound lean ground beef or turkey

5 Italian sausages (you can combine sweet and hot,
    about 1½ pounds total), casings removed

1 tablespoon Sofrito (page 158)

Salt and freshly ground black pepper

2 cups My Meaty Spaghetti Sauce (page 166) or your favorite
    tomato sauce

One 15-ounce container ricotta cheese

16 ounces (4 cups) shredded mozzarella cheese (or more!)

¼ cup freshly grated Parmesan cheese

¼ cup chopped fresh parsley leaves

1 Preheat the oven to 325°F. Bring a large pot of water to a boil.

2 Cook the pasta in the boiling water for 2 minutes less than the directions on the box indicate (you want it to be al dente), drain, and set aside.

3 Place the ground meat and sausage in a large saucepan over medium heat, cover, and cook, stirring occasionally with a wooden spoon or using a potato masher to break up the large chunks, until the ground meat is no longer pink and the sausage is cooked through, about 15 minutes. Stir in the sofrito and salt and pepper and continue cooking, covered, until it bubbles, another 3 to 5 minutes.

4. Turn off the heat. Uncover and drain most of the liquid (don't drain it all or the meat will dry up). Return the pot to the stove and stir in the sauce and ricotta cheese. Add the cooked pasta and mix well.

5. Spread the pasta mixture in a large baking pan or lasagna dish (9 by 13-inch baking pan is fine). Evenly sprinkle the mozzarella on top, followed by the Parmesan and parsley. Loosely cover the dish with foil and bake in the oven until the cheese is melted and the sauce is bubbling, about 20 minutes. Serve immediately.

Macarrones con Pollo *Macaroni with Chicken*

When I was growing up, Mami always kept macaroni on hand in case company came by; I've continued that custom. Pasta feeds many people, and it's quick and easy. This sofrito- and adobo-kissed chicken works beautifully with the pasta to make this Italian–Puerto Rican dish! I like rigatoni's large ridges and holes because it goes really well with meats (and chunky sauces). Enjoy with a leafy green salad, Plátanos Dulces (page 73), and Garlic Bread (page 172).

SERVES 4 TO 6

6 to 8 chicken pieces (2 to 2^1/$_2$ pounds), preferably drumsticks and thighs

2 teaspoons Adobo (page 164)

^{1}/$_4$ cup extra virgin olive oil

2 tablespoons Sofrito (page 158)

2 tablespoons tomato paste

^{1}/$_4$ cup pimiento-stuffed Spanish green olives

One 16-ounce box rigatoni pasta

^{1}/$_2$ teaspoon freshly ground black pepper

^{1}/$_4$ cup chopped fresh cilantro leaves

1 Bring a large pot of water to a boil. Using your hands, coat the chicken pieces with the adobo.

2 Heat the oil in a large skillet over medium heat. Stir in the sofrito, and heat through, about 2 minutes.

3 Add the chicken pieces and top with the tomato paste. Add the olives, cover, and cook, stirring occasionally, until the chicken is cooked through, about 30 minutes.

4 Meanwhile, cook the pasta according to the package instructions, drain, and set aside.

5 Just before serving, combine the chicken with the pasta, and sprinkle cilantro on top.

Picadillo de Carne Molida
Sofrito-Spiced Ground Beef Casserole

Picadillo could be translated into a phrase like "put it together and get it out!" but literally it means little pieces. Picadillo is used throughout the Americas to describe meat fillings for everything from empanadas to *papas* (potatoes); this Puerto Rican version is one that I originally had at the Cuchifritos—one of my favorite spots up on 116th Street in East Harlem—and I adapted for my own family. Ground beef is wonderful because not only is it foolproof and relatively inexpensive (and also quick cooking), it also blends well with a variety of vegetables and seasonings. I serve my picadillo on top of Basic White Rice (page 171), along with a leafy green salad.

SERVES 6

2 pounds lean ground beef
One 8-ounce can tomato sauce
1 tablespoon Sofrito (page 158)
Salt and freshly ground black pepper
2 large russet potatoes, peeled and diced into bite-size chunks
One 14.5 to 15-ounce can peas and carrots, or
  2 cups thawed frozen peas and carrots, drained

1 In a large skillet, cook the ground beef over medium heat, stirring frequently with a wooden spoon or using a potato masher to break up the large chunks, until it is browned, about 10 minutes.

2 Stir in the tomato sauce and sofrito. Add salt and pepper and mix well. Cover and cook until it starts to bubble, about 3 minutes.

3 Add the potatoes and stir well. Cover and continue simmering over low heat, stirring occasionally, until the potatoes are tender, about 10 minutes.

4 Uncover and add the peas and carrots. Let cook, stirring frequently, just until heated through, about 5 minutes. Serve immediately.

Pepper Steak

This is absolutely my mother's most popular "visitors'" dish; she usually makes it when the kids and I come by for dinner. She knows that when her grandsons are coming, it's time to make a large *caldero* of her pepper steak. Prior to our arrival, she picks up a large piece of meat from the market, and cuts it with the expertise of a trained butcher. Eric, Mark, Nicholas, and I all enjoy this dish with a bit of *pique* (Puerto Rican hot sauce) or Tabasco, and served over Basic White Rice (page 171), or Tostones (page 74).

SERVES 6

3 pounds sirloin, top, or bottom round steak, cut into $1/4$-inch-thick, 1-inch-long strips

1 teaspoon Sazón (page 163)

Salt and freshly ground black pepper

2 tablespoons soy sauce

$1/2$ cup canned tomato sauce

1 large red bell pepper, seeded and julienned (sliced into $1/8$-inch-thick, 1-inch-long strips)

1 large green bell pepper, seeded and julienned (sliced into $1/8$-inch-thick, 1-inch-long strips)

1 large yellow or orange bell pepper, seeded and julienned (sliced into $1/8$-inch-thick, 1-inch-long strips)

1 large Vidalia or Spanish onion, peeled and julienned (sliced into $1/8$-inch-thick, 1-inch-long strips)

2 tablespoons gravy browning sauce or 1 teaspoon all-purpose flour

1 Season the steak with the sazón and salt and pepper to taste. Place the meat into a large skillet over medium-high heat. Cover and cook until the meat starts to brown, about 5 minutes. Then cover and cook until the steam starts to create a broth, about 5 more minutes.

2 Add the soy sauce and tomato sauce and stir well. Cover and cook until the sauce starts to boil, about 3 minutes.

3 Add the peppers, onion, and browning sauce. Stir well and cover. Cook until the onions and peppers are tender, about 10 minutes. Serve immediately.

Bistec Encebollado   *Steak with Onions*

No matter whether it's a Cuban, Dominican, or Puerto Rican restaurant, my favorite dish is always *bistec encebollado*. Though the preparation may be somewhat different, the heart and soul of this dish is the same. Serve with Basic White Rice (page 171), Habichuelas Rosadas (page 48), and Plátanos Dulces (page 73). I also like this dish with salsa—the sauce *and* the music!

SERVES 4

4 thin-cut skirt steaks (about 2 pounds)

1 tablespoon Adobo (page 164)

2 medium onions, peeled and sliced into $1/4$-inch-thick rings

2 garlic cloves, peeled and minced

One 8-ounce can tomato sauce

1 Heat a large skillet over low heat. Season the steaks with adobo on both sides and the place them in the skillet. Cover and cook until the steaks start to brown and liquid starts to form from the steam, about 15 minutes.

2 Add the onions, garlic, and tomato sauce. Let the steak and vegetable mixture simmer until the onions are tender, about 10 minutes. Serve immediately.

Burgers, My Way

When I was growing up, our dinners were usually different rice dishes. But every once in a while, Mami would prepare a special school-night treat: burgers! They offered a welcome and delicious break from our typical meals. I've carried on the tradition, only made the burgers with some of my own spice. My kids and their friends love these, and I hope you will, too! Serve these burgers with Yuca Frita (page 79).

MAKES 6 BURGERS

2 pounds lean ground beef

1 large onion, peeled and finely diced

$1/_4$ cup chopped fresh cilantro leaves

1 teaspoon salt

1 teaspoon garlic powder

$1/_2$ teaspoon red pepper flakes

Freshly ground black pepper

6 burger buns

Cheese and ketchup, for serving (optional)

1. In a large bowl combine the beef, onion, cilantro, salt, garlic powder, red pepper flakes, and black pepper. Use your hands or a wooden spoon to mix until well blended. Cover and refrigerate for at least 40 minutes or overnight.

2. Heat a grill pan, skillet, or grill to medium heat. Divide the meat into 6 portions. Roll each portion in your palm until you form a large meatball. Flatten it to make a patty.

3. Cook until browned on both sides and to the desired doneness on the inside, about 15 minutes all together for medium, or to your desired doneness.

4. Meanwhile, lightly toast the buns. Serve the burgers on the buns and have guests add cheese and/or ketchup as desired.

Shepherd's Pie

This is my version of the classic British dish. The first time I saw it, I was at an old friend's house; she was about to make it for a family function. Just one look told me how easy it was—but for me, it was missing *el sabor puertoriqueño* (the Puerto Rican flavor). So, I remedied that with a bit of sofrito! My family loves this dish—and I like it because it's so easy, not to mention tasty.

SERVES 6

Instant mashed potato flakes for 6 servings

1 pound lean ground beef

One 8-ounce can tomato sauce

1 tablespoon Sofrito (page 158)

1 cup thawed frozen peas and carrots, or one 8.5-ounce can, drained

1 cup thawed frozen corn kernels, or one 8.75-ounce can, drained

Nonstick cooking spray

4 tablespoons ($^1/_2$ stick) unsalted butter

Salt and freshly ground black pepper

1. Prepare the instant mashed potatoes according to the directions on the box, and set aside.

2. Preheat the broiler.

3. In a medium skillet over medium heat, add the beef and cook, stirring constantly with a wooden spoon or using a potato masher to break up the large chunks, until it's completely cooked (not pink at all), about 15 minutes.

4. Drain the meat of any liquid and return the meat to the pan. Add the tomato sauce and sofrito and continue cooking, stirring occasionally, until heated through, 3 to 5 minutes.

5   In a bowl, combine the peas and carrots with the corn. Set aside.

6   Assemble the pie: Coat a 9 by 13-inch baking dish with cooking spray. Spoon the meat mixture into the baking dish and spread it in an even layer on the bottom. Use the same technique to top it with a layer of the vegetable mixture. Add the mashed potatoes on top and, using the back of the spoon or a butter knife, spread it as best you can.

7   Thinly slice the butter and distribute it evenly on top of the potatoes. Place the pan into the broiler and cook until the mashed potatoes have a nice brown color on top, about 5 minutes. Sprinkle with salt and pepper. Divide into squares and serve.

Puerto Rican Stuffed Meatloaf

Ray has always loved meatloaf, and this is his absolute favorite. The sofrito and sazón add the Puerto Rican touches; I added the spinach and cheese because I wanted it to be healthier—and I like those flavors a lot! Serve this meatloaf with Basic White Rice (page 171), a leafy green salad, and Garlic Bread (page 172). If you have any leftovers, they make a great sandwich on Italian or your favorite bread.

SERVES 6

$^1/_2$ pound ground chicken

$^1/_2$ pound ground pork

$^1/_2$ pound ground beef

2 tablespoons garlic powder

2 teaspoons Sazón (page 163)

Salt and freshly ground black pepper

1 tablespoon Sofrito (page 158)

Half a 10-ounce bag fresh spinach, well rinsed and dried,
  and coarsely chopped

4 ounces (1 cup) shredded whole mozzarella cheese

$^1/_4$ cup chopped fresh cilantro leaves

Nonstick cooking spray

$^1/_4$ cup ketchup

1 Preheat the oven to 350°F.

2 In a large bowl, combine the chicken, beef, and pork. Use your hands to mix them well. Season with the garlic powder and sazón, and salt and pepper. Mix in the sofrito.

3 Spread a sheet of wax paper on a work surface. Transfer the seasoned meat to the wax paper and shape into an 8 by 5-inch loaf. Make a

lengthwise well, about 2 inches deep and $^{1}/_{2}$ inch wide, running length of the loaf, in the middle of the meat mixture using your hand or a wooden spoon. Place the spinach in a layer in the well, then the mozzarella, and finally the cilantro.

4 Seal the well using the meat mixture; you don't want any of the stuffing to stick out. Transfer into a spray-coated 9 by 13-inch baking pan. Spread the ketchup over the top.

5 Cover loosely with foil and bake until mostly cooked through (a quick cut on the top should reveal meat that is no longer pink), 45 to 50 minutes. Remove the foil and bake until the top is browned, another 10 to 15 minutes.

6 Let rest for about 10 minutes, then slice and serve.

Pernil *Roast Pork*

Pernil is synonymous with Puerto Rican tradition; it is the main meat dish on Christmas, New Year's Eve, and many other special occasions. On one such occasion my brother Jay tried to be a rebel and make roast duck. Of course the meal was delicious, but when it was served, everyone looked around for the pernil! Since then, on important holidays—to the delight and expectations of family members and friends—I haven't strayed from our highly anticipated main dish. Though it's easy to prepare, you should start about 48 hours ahead of time with the marination process. Serve your Pernil with Arroz con Gandules (page 95) or Guineos Sancochados (page 47).

SERVES 6 TO 8

1¹/₂ cups extra virgin olive oil

4 teaspoons salt

4 teaspoons freshly ground black pepper

2 teaspoons Sazón (page 163)

6 to 8 pounds pork shoulder in one piece, with skin

4 garlic cloves, peeled and crushed

1 tablespoon dried oregano

1 Two days before you plan to serve, whisk together 1 cup of the oil, 3 teaspoons salt, 3 teaspoons pepper, and 1 teaspoon of the sazón. Place the pork in a dish and cover it with the marinade. Cover tightly and refrigerate for 48 hours, turning occasionally to ensure the meat is evenly coated.

2 Preheat the oven to 350°F.

3 In a medium bowl, whisk together the remaining ¹/₂ cup oil, the garlic, oregano, and the remaining teaspoons of sazón, salt, and pepper. Place the pork shoulder in a roasting pan. Using a sharp knife, poke eight to ten ¹/₄-inch deep pockets all over the pork. Pour the olive oil mixture all over the meat, using your hands to make sure it's evenly distributed and the pockets are filled with the seasoning.

4 Bake the pork, skin side up, until the skin is crispy and the meat reaches a temperature of at least 160°F on an instant-read thermometer, 4 to 6 hours. (You'll also know when meat is done when you don't see any pink and it's easily sliced.) Let rest for 10 minutes before carving. Serve hot.

Stuffed Pork Loin

Eating any meal at Ray's mom's house always means being fed until you can't possibly eat any more, but I'll never forget the first time Mercedes made me this dish. We walked into the kitchen and saw the cook in action. Ray and I looked on as his mom aggressively stabbed the pork loin—making holes in the meat she was about to stuff—and he was slightly taken aback. "Mom, what are you doing to that poor thing?" he asked, half embarrassed as he saw me with a quizzical expression. Mercedes waved him out of the kitchen, but thankfully called me in to teach me how to make her fabulous Italian sausage, garlic, and chorizo stuffing. Serve with Arroz con Gandules (page 95), and a leafy green salad.

SERVES 6

2 sweet Italian sausage links (about $1/4$ pound)

2 chorizo links (4 to 5 ounces; see Note)

2 garlic cloves, peeled

2 tablespoons extra virgin olive oil

One 2-pound whole boneless pork loin

1 Remove the sausage and chorizo meat from their casings, and cook in a large skillet over medium heat until browned, 10 to 12 minutes; use a wooden spoon or potato masher to break up the larger chunks and prevent the meat from sticking. Remove from the heat, drain the fat, and set aside.

2 Drop the garlic into a *pilón* or a wooden bowl about 2 to 3 inches wide, and mash with a pestle. (If you don't have a pestle, use the back of a wooden spoon.) Pour the oil on top of the garlic and stir to combine.

3 Place the roast, fat side down, on a clean surface. With a sharp knife, poke eight to ten 1-inch-deep holes (they should be deep enough to allow the filling in) along the length of the pork loin. Stuff the holes with the meat mixture. Using a spoon and your hand, spread the mashed garlic over the entire piece of meat. Place the roast in a shallow baking dish, holes side up. Cover with clear wrap and let the meat marinate in the refrigerator for an hour.

4 Preheat the oven to 325°F.

5 Remove the plastic, cover the meat loosely with foil, and place the pan in the oven. Cook until the meat starts to turn brown, about 30 minutes. Remove the foil, baste the pork with liquid in the pan, and cook until crisp on the outside, and an instant-read thermometer inserted into the pork (but not in the stuffing) registers 160°F.

6 Let the pork rest for about 15 minutes before serving.

NOTE: Chorizo is available in Latin American groceries, as well as some larger supermarkets and butchers.

Jamón con Azúcar Negra y Piña Tostada

Baked Ham with Brown Sugar and Roasted Pineapple

Though *Pernil* (page 134) is the star of our Christmas and Thanksgiving dinners, baked ham certainly plays a supporting role! *Jamón con azúcar negra* makes appearances all year round at birthdays, christenings, and many other celebrations. Everyone in my family loves the flavors of the ham and sugar, and the lightly crunchy caramelized pineapple slices that rest on top—and the red cherries that add both color and more sugar. (My brother Jay, the health buff, kids us about the sugar rush that comes after eating this sweet ham!) When my sister Linda and I (we're the super sugar fans!) first made this dish, we used canned ham—though now we both use fresh spiral-sliced ham. This meal is simple to prepare and adaptable; it can be served hot or at room temperature.

SERVES 10 TO 12

1 cup dark brown sugar

Extra virgin olive oil

One 6- to 8-pound spiral-sliced ham (canned ham is fine, too)

Four 8-ounce cans pineapple slices in light syrup

Toothpicks

$^1/_2$ cup drained maraschino cherries (optional)

1 Preheat oven to 325°F.

2 Combine the sugar and $^1/_2$ cup water in a sauce pan and cook over low heat, stirring constantly, until the sugar dissolves, about 5 minutes.

3 Grease the bottom of a roasting pan with a drizzle of olive oil, and place the ham in it. Using a basting brush, coat the ham with the sugar. Cover the pan with the lid or seal tightly with aluminum foil. Cook until the ham is heated through, about 40 minutes.

4 Use the basting brush to collect the sugar now on the bottom of the pan, and baste the ham. Pour the juice of two of the cans of pineapple into the bottom of the roasting pan. Place some of the pineapple slices right on top of the ham and use toothpicks to secure them. (If you're using the cherries, also attach them with toothpicks inside the pineapple slices.) The rest of the fruit can sit on the bottom of the pan. Baste again, return the ham to the oven, and cook uncovered until the pineapple is golden brown, about 15 minutes.

5 Slice and serve hot or at room temperature. (Leftovers—if there are any—can be refrigerated and made into sandwiches on the following day.)

Fried Pork with Green Bananas

Fried pork and green bananas are two of the key players in Puerto Rican cuisine. As is the case of most of the meat dishes I grew up with, this meat is ideally marinated overnight before cooking. Having the meat soak in these fabulous flavors adds depth of taste and also enhances the texture of the meat. This dish can be served as an appetizer, or as a main dish with Arroz con Gandules (page 95) and a leafy green salad.

SERVES 4

2 pounds pork tenderloins, diced into $^1/_2$-inch cubes

1 tablespoon Adobo (page 164)

1 tablespoon Sofrito (page 158)

4 to 6 green bananas

Salt

Vegetable oil

$^1/_4$ cup Mojito (page 159)

Freshly ground black pepper

1 The day before you plan to serve, place the pork cubes in a bowl. Stir in the adobo and sofrito and mix well so that the pieces are well coated. Cover and refrigerate overnight.

2 On the following day, prepare the green bananas: Soak them in warm water in a large bowl (or in the sink) for about 20 minutes; this will soften the skin and make peeling easier. Remove the bananas from the water, dry them, cut the ends off, and cut a slit lengthwise down the middle. Open and remove the peel, using a knife or your hands, as if you were taking a jacket off somebody. Cut the bananas into 1-inch pieces.

3 Fill a stockpot about halfway with water and bring to a boil over high heat. Add the bananas and 1 teaspoon salt to the pot. Simmer until the bananas are tender, about 20 minutes. Drain and set aside. Drizzle some vegetable oil on them so they don't dry up.

4 In a heavy skillet or deep fryer, add about 1 inch of oil and heat over high until it's very hot. Fry the pork pieces, turning as needed, until they're dark brown and crispy on all sides, about 15 minutes total. Drain on paper towels.

5 To serve, place a few pieces of pork on a plate with a few banana pieces. Top with a drizzle of mojito and a sprinkling of salt and pepper.

Vinaigrette Marinated T-Bone Steaks

After years of experimenting with many foods from my childhood, I learned there are so many ways of putting flavors together, and that sometimes the answer to great taste combinations lies right in the cupboard! This extremely no-fuss recipe clearly illustrates my point. Made with my Lemon Vinaigrette Dressing (page 161), which I always have in the fridge, this marinated steak dinner satisfies all the meat-loving men (seven!) in my home—and me, too! In the summer we grill the steaks outside (my favorite way of preparing them), but in the winter we broil them. Serve with Tostones (page 74) or Plátanos Dulces (page 73).

SERVES 6

Two 2-pound (1¹/₂-inch-thick) T-bone steaks
2 cups Elsie's Lemon Vinaigrette (page 161)

1 Place the steaks in a single layer in a deep baking dish. Pour the vinaigrette over them, making sure they're well coated. Cover and let marinate in the refrigerator for at least 2 hours (or even overnight).

2 Heat a grill or grill pan to high. Cook the steaks, turning over once. For rare, cook 9 to 11 minutes; 12 to 14 minutes total for medium-well, and 16 minutes total for well-done.

3 Let stand, uncovered, for 10 minutes before slicing. Then cut the steaks into serving portions.

Chuletas con Piña
Pork Chops with Pineapple

Like many of my contemporaries, I grew up with *The Brady Bunch* —and will never forget Peter Brady's famous pork chops and applesauce! The Brady Bunch seemed to be the quintessential American family, and yet pork chops were (are!) such a part of my Puerto Rican heritage. I have always loved the combination of the savory and sweet—but enjoy the tropical kiss of pineapple and the additional *toque puertoriqueño* (Puerto Rican touch) of adobo. Serve with Basic White Rice (page 171) and a leafy green salad.

SERVES 4

Vegetable oil

8 medium bone-in pork chops (not loin and not too thick)

2 tablespoons Adobo (page 164)

Two 8-ounce can pineapple rings, packed in light syrup

1. Preheat the oven to 325°F. Coat the bottom of a baking pan with a layer of vegetable oil.

2. Season each side of the pork chops with adobo; use your fingers to spread it around. Lay the chops side by side on the baking pan. Cover the chops with foil and bake until they're no longer pink, about 20 minutes.

3. Remove the cover, drain any excess liquid, and top the chops with the pineapple slices. Pour the pineapple juice (leftover syrup in the cans) on top of the chops. Raise the heat to 350°F, and bake the chops, uncovered, until the pineapple slices are slightly brown, about 15 minutes. Serve on a platter topped with the juices in the pan.

Chuletas de Puerco con Aceite de Hojas de Laurel y Vegetales
Pork Chops with Bay Leaf Oil and Vegetables

I'm not sure if *mi mamá* (my mom), when she added this herb to many of her dishes, was aware of the bay leaf's noble history! Legend surrounded the *hojas de laurel* (bay leaves) even before champions of the first Olympic Games, in 776 BC, were crowned with wreaths of the shiny, fragrant green leaf. In this simple and tasty pork chop dish, a version of what I grew up with, I've added the touch of this wonderful herb cooked briefly in oil, which enhances both its flavor and fragrance. Serve this dish with Tostones (page 74) or Yuca Frita (page 78).

SERVES 6

2 tablespoons olive oil

6 to 8 thin-cut bone-in rib pork chops

1 tablespoon Adobo (page 164)

1 teaspoon Sazón (page 163)

4 dried bay leaves

2 medium onions, peeled and sliced lengthwise into $1/4$-inch-wide strips

1 large red bell pepper, seeded and sliced lengthwise into $1/4$-inch-wide strips

1 large green bell pepper, seeded and sliced lengthwise into $1/4$-inch-wide strips

2 cups coarsely chopped beefsteak tomatoes

1 Preheat the oven to 325°F.

2 Coat the bottom of a roasting pan with about 1 teaspoon of the oil. Lay the pork chops down flat in a dish and season them with adobo and sazón on both sides. Transfer them to the pan. Cover the pan with the lid or seal tightly with aluminum foil and bake until the chops are cooked through, about 25 minutes.

3 Meanwhile, heat the remaining oil in a large skillet over medium heat. Add the bay leaves and cook until fragrant, 2 to 3 minutes. Add the onions, peppers, and tomatoes and cook, stirring occasionally, until the peppers and onions are softened, about 10 minutes.

4 Spoon the vegetable mixture on top of the chops. Let the mixture rest for about 10 minutes (to let flavors soak in) before serving.

Higado con Tocino *Liver with Bacon*

Liver was not something we kids were initially excited about—at all. Despite the fact that Papi used to remind us *"es bueno para su salud,"* (it's good for you), it took even more convincing on the part of my parents to get us to eat it. But, then we did—and we liked it! I think it was the combination of flavors and textures that won us over. So, even if you weren't previously a liver fan, I urge you to try this tasty—and very simple—dish. Serve with Basic White Rice (page 171) or rice and beans.

SERVES 4

1 pound hickory-smoked bacon

Two 1-pound liver steaks

2 tablespoons extra virgin olive oil

1 large Vidalia onion, peeled and sliced into $1/4$-inch-thick rings

Salt and freshly ground black pepper

1 Preheat the oven to 325°F.

2 Separate the bacon into two equal parts; half you'll use on one steak and half on the other. Take the bacon strips, and wrap them, horizontally, around the steaks. Repeat until you've used up all the bacon.

3 Drizzle 1 tablespoon of oil on the bottom of a baking pan large enough to hold both liver steaks; use a pastry brush to evenly coat the pan. Place the wrapped steaks in the pan, and top them with the onion rings. Drizzle the rest of the oil over the steaks and onions, season with salt and pepper, cover with foil, and bake until the onions get soft and the bacon is slightly cooked, about 20 minutes.

4 Uncover and bake until the bacon is crispy, about 15 minutes. Drain. Serve immediately.

Camarones con Chorizo al Ajillo *Garlic Shrimp and Sausage*

Cooking should be about experimenting and trying new things, which is something that I love to do. Sometimes I like to take the basic ingredients I use and combine them in ways I may have never tried before; that's how I created this dish. I combined chorizo—a slightly spicy sausage—with a bit of onion and garlic, along with another favorite: shrimp. When Mami tried this years ago, she really liked it, and so I've been making it ever since. Serve this dish over Tostones (page 74) or Basic White Rice (page 171).

SERVES 6

3 teaspoons extra virgin olive oil

4 to 5 large chorizo links (about 1 pound), diced in $1/4$-inch cubes (see Note)

1 small onion, peeled and finely diced

2 garlic cloves, peeled and finely diced

2 pounds peeled and deveined large shrimp (thawed if frozen)

Freshly ground black pepper

1. Pour 1 teaspoon of the olive oil (this is just to start the chorizo, which can be a little oily but you don't want it to burn) into a large skillet and heat over medium heat. Add the chorizo and stir well. Cook, stirring occasionally, until it starts to brown, about 5 minutes.

2. Add the onion and garlic and mix well. Cover again and cook, stirring occasionally, until the onions start to soften, about 5 minutes.

3. Uncover the skillet, add the shrimp, raise the heat to high, and let the mixture start to sizzle. Continue cooking, stirring frequently to coat the shrimp with the chorizo, until the shrimp are pink, about 5 minutes.

4. Transfer the mixture to a bowl, drizzle with the remaining 2 teaspoons oil, and season with pepper. Serve immediately.

NOTE: Chorizo is available in Latin American groceries, as well as some larger supermarkets and butchers.

Mofongo con Camarones *Mashed Fried Plantains Stuffed with Shrimp*

Every Puerto Rican knows what *mofongo* is! Though ingredients may vary from town to town—and even family to family—the heart and soul of mofongo, mashed fried green plantains, remains the same. Though this is a lot of work, it's definitely worth it.

SERVES 6

1 tablespoon vegetable oil, plus extra for frying

1 small onion, peeled and finely diced

One 7 to 8-ounce jar roasted pimientos, drained and finely diced

1 medium tomato, seeded and diced

1 teaspoon Sazón (page 163)

2 pounds peeled, deveined, and cooked medium shrimp (thawed if frozen)

$^{1}/_{2}$ cup canned tomato sauce

6 to 8 green plantains

1 head garlic, separated into cloves and peeled

Salt

1 Heat the oil in a skillet over medium heat. Add the onions and cook, stirring frequently, until they become transparent, about 5 minutes.

2 Stir in the pimientos, tomato, and sazón. Cover and cook over low heat until the mixture starts to bubble, about 5 minutes.

3 Add the shrimp and tomato sauce and stir well. Cover and simmer, stirring from time to time, until the shrimp is warm and the sauce is well blended, about 5 minutes. Remove from the heat and set aside.

4 Prepare the plantains: Soak them in warm water in a large bowl (or in the sink) for about 20 minutes; this will soften the skin and make peeling easier. Remove the plantains from the water, dry them, cut the ends off, and cut a slit lengthwise down the middle. Open and remove the peel, using a knife or your hands, as if you were taking a jacket off somebody. Cut them on the diagonal into $^1/_2$-inch chunks.

5 Add about 2 inches of vegetable oil to another skillet—it should be enough to submerge the plantain pieces—and heat over high heat. Fry the plantain pieces without crowding them in the pan, until golden, 3 to 5 minutes on each side. Remove the plantains to drain on paper towels, but reserve the oil. Repeat with the remaining plantain pieces, if necessary.

6 Drop the garlic into a *pilón* or a wooden bowl 2 to 3 inches wide, and mash it with a pestle. (If you don't have a pestle, use the back of a wooden spoon.) Add a dash of salt. Remove the mashed garlic and set aside.

7 Take a tablespoon of the hot oil from the skillet and coat the inside of the pilón with it (this will keep the plantain from sticking). Add 3 or 4 fried plantain slices, along with $^1/_2$ teaspoon of crushed garlic, and mash together until you've formed a lining—like a cup—inside the pilón. (If it's not mashing together well, add more oil.) Once you have created the cup, put 1 or 2 tablespoons of the shrimp mixture in the center (you want to fill it with the shrimp).

8 Here comes the tricky part: Cover the top of the pilón with a small, flat serving plate, and flip it so that the open side is upside down. Carefully lift off the pilón. It should look like a small mound. To serve, ladle a bit of the shrimp mixture on top.

NOTE: If your plantain cup doesn't come out easily the first time, try oiling a butter knife and gently scraping it around the outer edges—as you would with a cake mold—so that the plantain doesn't stick to the pilón.

Camarones en Cerveza   *Shrimp Cooked in Beer*

Shrimp and beer are music to my ears! *Una cerveza fría* (an ice-cold beer) is what many of us look forward to after a hard day's work. But beer is not only great to drink; it's also wonderful to cook with. My sister Melissa adds beer to her ham before she bakes it, but I decided to combine my cerveza with my *camarones*. So grownups, take a sip, and start this recipe. Serve with Tostones (page 74).

SERVES 6

1/2 cup (1 stick) unsalted butter

1 medium green bell pepper, seeded and julienned
   (sliced into 1/8-inch-thick, 1-inch-long strips)

1 large onion, peeled and julienned
   (sliced into 1/8-inch-thick, 1-inch-long strips)

2 pounds peeled and deveined medium shrimp (thawed if frozen)

1/2 cup beer (any type is fine)

Red pepper flakes (optional)

Salt and freshly ground black pepper

1. In a large skillet over medium heat, melt the butter. Add the green pepper and cook, stirring frequently, until it starts to soften, about 5 minutes. Add the onion and cook, stirring frequently, until it starts to soften, about 5 minutes.

2. Add the shrimp to the skillet and raise the heat to high. Cook until the shrimp start to turn pink, about 1 minute. Pour in the beer, bring to a boil, then reduce the heat to medium and let simmer until cooked through, about 5 minutes.

3. Using a strainer or a ladle, remove the shrimp, onions, and peppers and put them into a bowl and cover to keep warm. Let the remaining

liquid in the skillet cook until it's reduced by half, about another 5 minutes. (At this point you can add red pepper flakes to the liquid for a spicy kick.)

2 Pour the liquid over the shrimp and vegetable mixture, season with salt and pepper, and serve.

Piononos
Plantain Rolls Stuffed with Spiced Ground Beef

The name of this dish has an interesting story: Apparently Pope Pío IX, who lived during the nineteenth century, was also called Pío No No. A baker in Spain created a small, short, and round dulce de leche–filled rolled-up pastry (super sweet and much loved by many) that was said to resemble this pope's silhouette. Now, though the name and shape are somewhat similar, I'm not sure how *piononos* traveled to Puerto Rico, nor how the ingredients were so changed! At any rate, I'm sharing with you here these well-known plantain-shelled meat treats that I grew up with. Like the Pastelón de Plátano (page120), this truly Puerto Rican dish has a unique look and flavor. Serve your piononos with a leafy green salad on the side for a fabulously different—and delicious—meal.

SERVES 4

1 pound ground beef

$^1/_2$ cup canned tomato sauce

1 teaspoon Sofrito (page 158)

1 teaspoon Sazón (page 163)

$^1/_4$ cup drained pimiento-stuffed Spanish green olives, coarsely chopped

4 ripe plantains (yellow with minimal black spots)

$^1/_4$ cup vegetable oil, plus extra for frying

2 large eggs

Salt and freshly ground black pepper

1. In a skillet over medium heat, add the beef and cook, stirring occasionally to break it up, until it's browned, about 10 minutes. Stir in the tomato sauce, sofrito, and sazón and mix well. Add the olives. Cook until the mixture starts to boil, about 5 minutes. Remove from the heat and set aside.

2. Prepare the plantains: Cut the ends off and cut a slit lengthwise down the middle. Open and remove the peel, using a knife or your hands, as if you were taking a jacket off somebody. Slice the plan-

tains lengthwise into about 4 long, thin slices each. Heat just enough oil, about a tablespoon, to coat the bottom of a large skillet over medium heat. Fry the plantain slices in batches, adding more oil as needed, until golden, about 3 minutes on each side. Drain on paper towels.

3. Meanwhile, take one plantain slice and lay it flat. Scoop a heaping tablespoon of the meat mixture on the end closest to you, and start rolling the plantain with the meat inside so that it forms a small roll. Use a toothpick to keep it closed and don't worry, some meat might fall out! Repeat with the remaining plantain slices and meat filling.

4. Add vegetable oil to a deep skillet to a depth of 2 inches and heat over medium heat.

5. Beat the eggs in a bowl and set aside. Dip each of the rolls into the eggs and using a large slotted spoon, carefully place them into the hot oil. Fry on all sides until the rolls are fully cooked, about 7 minutes all together. Drain on paper towels, and serve immediately.

French Toast with Cheese

My *Tía Paulina* (Aunt Paulina) was like a second mom to me in many ways. Since she was my mom's sister, we spent a lot of time with her and her girls—especially during the summer. Though not as fluent as Mom in the kitchen, Paulina came up with some offbeat yet tasty creations, like this French toast. Now I make it at home and my boys just love it, as I think you will, too!

SERVES 6

6 large eggs

¹/₄ teaspoon ground cinnamon

2 drops vanilla extract

12 slices white or whole wheat bread

6 slices Cheddar or American cheese

Unsalted butter

Maple syrup

1. Combine the eggs, cinnamon, and vanilla in a dish deep enough to dip the bread into (1 or 2 pieces at a time) and mix until blended.

2. In a large skillet, melt enough butter to coat the pan over medium heat. Coat both sides of four slices of bread with the egg mixture and let them drain slightly over the dish. Add the bread to the skillet (if your pan is too small, you may have to do this in batches) and cook until the egg mixture is lightly browned on one side, about 3 minutes. Flip them and put one slice of cheese on top of two of the browned sides. Top those slices with the other two pieces, toasted side down. When the bottom pieces are browned, after about 3 minutes, flip the sandwiches and continue cooking until lightly browned on the other side, about 3 minutes more. The toast is ready when both sides are golden and the cheese is melted. Repeat with the

remaining slices. (You can let the toast rest in a 200°F oven until you're finished making all the sandwiches.)

3 To serve, place each sandwich on a plate. Drizzle the French toast with syrup, and serve immediately.

Basics

These fundamental and easy-to-put-together recipes are the backbone for my style of cooking; you'll notice that most of my dishes cannot be created without them. Of course, many of the products of these basic recipes can be store-bought (which isn't bad if you're stuck—and I'm the first to confess that I've bought the store versions on occasion!), but they're simple enough to make up fresh, without the preservatives and artificial ingredients. Once you start using sofrito, sazón, and adobo—and the others—I'm sure you'll find ways of using them to jazz up other dishes you make. And in time you'll realize, as I have, that life is much more exciting with spice!

Sofrito   *Puerto Rican Pepper Sauce*

This sauce, one that's a basic for many of recipes in this book, was taught to me as a young girl by my mom. In fact, if you open my refrigerator on any day, you will most likely find it there. The flavor of the peppers, onion, garlic—and of course cilantro—is magical. Add a tablespoon of this concoction to your soups, stews, grilled meats—just about anything—and the enhanced flavors will thrill your family and friends!

MAKES ABOUT 2 CUPS

2 large Spanish onions, peeled and quartered

1 large green pepper, seeded and quartered

1 large red bell pepper, seeded and quartered

1 bunch cilantro leaves (the more the merrier)

2 heads garlic, separated into cloves and peeled

Combine all of the ingredients in a food processor fitted with a steel blade. Process until well blended; the sofrito should have the consistency of tomato puree. Transfer to a glass or plastic container, cover, and store in the refrigerator for up to 4 weeks.

Mojito
Traditional Garlic Dipping Sauce

Sure, you may have heard of the fabulous cocktail by the same name—made with fresh mint leaves, lime juice, and rum—but you may not be familiar with this fabulous sauce. Any Puerto Rican or Cuban will tell you that they only like their *tostones* with *mojito*; this sauce also spices up just about any meat dish, and works as a marinade with pork chops and steak, too. Once you make it, I'm sure you'll find ways to incorporate it into your repertoire.

MAKES ABOUT 1¹/₂ CUPS

2 heads garlic, separated into cloves and peeled
Salt
¹/₄ cup white vinegar
1 cup corn or vegetable oil
Freshly ground black pepper
Pinch of chopped fresh parsley leaves

1 Crush the garlic in a *pilón*, using a pestle and a bit of salt to grip the garlic. (If you don't have a pilón, you can use a bowl and the back of a wooden spoon, or a garlic press.)

2 In a glass container or empty jar with a cover, add the vinegar and the oil. Add the crushed garlic, a bit more salt, pepper to taste, and the parsley. Shake vigorously for about 3 minutes.

3 Use immediately, or refrigerate until ready to use or for up to 1 week. Be sure to mix again just before using, so that every spoonful has garlic.

Mojito Rojo   *Red Garlic Sauce*

I call this basic sauce *mojito rojo* because, though it has the addition of ketchup and mayonnaise, it has garlic and oil like its cousin. Serve this sauce with Arañitas (page 75), and any other treat you can think of! However, unlike the classic mojito, this should be used immediately and not stored.

MAKES 1 CUP

4 garlic cloves, peeled

Salt

$^1/_2$ cup mayonnaise

$^1/_2$ cup ketchup

1 tablespoon extra virgin olive oil

1 teaspoon white vinegar

1 Crush the garlic in a *pilón*, using a pestle and a bit of salt to grip the garlic. (If you don't have a pilón, you can use a bowl and the back of a wooden spoon or a garlic press.)

2 Combine the mayonnaise, ketchup, oil, and vinegar in a bowl and stir well to mix. Add the crushed garlic and stir again. Taste and add salt as needed. Serve immediately.

Elsie's Lemon Vinaigrette

Whether you're using this for a salad or meat marinade, this easy-to-prepare condiment is perfect! This is ideally prepared a day in advance (so that the flavors can meld), but I have also made it on the spur of the moment.

MAKES ABOUT 1 CUP

$^3/_4$ cup extra virgin olive oil

$^1/_4$ cup white vinegar

1 teaspoon fresh lemon juice

1 garlic glove, peeled and minced

$^1/_2$ small onion, peeled and minced

1 teaspoon chopped fresh cilantro leaves

$^1/_2$ teaspoon salt

$^1/_4$ teaspoon freshly ground black pepper

In a glass jar or bowl, whisk together the olive oil, vinegar, and lemon juice. Add the garlic, onion, cilantro, salt and pepper and whisk until well blended. Serve immediately, or cover and store in the refrigerator for up to 1 week.

Achiote Oil

In addition to my all-time favorite sazón, this is my very traditional and much-loved natural food coloring. Made with the rich red annatto seeds (which Mami and my aunts could pick from their backyards in Puerto Rico), this oil has a subtle, earthy aroma and colors many of our traditional treats—like Alcapurrias (page 64), Bacalaítos (page 62), and many rice dishes and stews. This oil should not be refrigerated, but kept covered at room temperature with your other oils.

MAKES 1 CUP

1 cup vegetable oil

3 to 4 tablespoons annatto seeds (see Note)

1 Pour the oil into a small saucepan and heat over medium heat (you don't want it to get too hot or it will burn the seeds). Once the oil is hot but not smoking, add about 3 tablespoons of the annatto seeds (the more seeds you use, the darker the oil will be and the less you'll have to use!).

2 Stir continuously until the oil turns a rich brownish-red color, about 2 minutes. Let cool to room temperature and strain the oil into a glass jar with a lid. Use immediately, or cover and store for up to 1 week.

NOTE: Annatto seeds can be found in Latin American groceries, as well as some large supermarkets.

Sazón *Traditional Puerto Rican Seasoning*

Sazón is a key ingredient in so many Puerto Rican dishes; I don't think we could live without it! Of course you can find sazón in little packets in the market—and they're certainly convenient—but I like to make my own version, which is simple and quite tasty—and doesn't have any artificial preservatives. I use equal amounts of the ingredients so that one doesn't overpower another.

**MAKES ABOUT
2 TABLESPOONS**

1 teaspoon paprika

1 teaspoon freshly ground black pepper

1 teaspoon saffron threads

1 teaspoon salt

1 teaspoon garlic powder

Mix all the seasonings together in a small bowl or jar. Using the tip of your finger, give it a taste and adjust seasonings as needed. Use immediately, or transfer to a small glass or plastic container, cover, and store for the next day; it's best made as close to using time as possible.

Adobo

Adobo is probably one of the most commonly used seasonings in Puerto Rican dishes (next to sofrito, of course). The combination of the different dry seasonings offers a multitude of flavors. Don't get me wrong: I'm still a fan of the store-bought versions, but I have run out on occasion, and so created my own, which you can store in a dry cool place for weeks. I use this adobo to season meat—even for future meals. On the weekends, when I'm trying to get a head start on the week's meals, I pack my adobo-covered meat into freezer bags, and then thaw and cook for a tasty and easy weeknight meal.

MAKES ABOUT 2 TABLESPOONS

2 teaspoons salt

2 teaspoons whole black peppercorns

2 teaspoons garlic powder

$^1/_2$ teaspoon dried oregano

Crush all ingredients in a pilón using a pestle, or in a bowl with the back of a wooden spoon. For a finer grain, sift the mixture through a strainer. Use immediately, or transfer to a small glass or plastic container, cover, and store for up to several weeks.

My Favorite Salsa

While making chicken cutlets one evening, I was looking for something to spruce them up a bit and discovered that I didn't have any jarred salsa in the house, so I decided to make my own. After experimenting a bit, this is what I came up with. Of course, you can find plenty of salsas on supermarket shelves these days, but I find many of the store-bought ones to be too sweet. This salsa is simple and healthy. I like to serve it over chicken cutlets, fish, oven omelets. I'm sure that once you try it you will find many ways to use it, as I have.

MAKES 2 CUPS

3 medium ripe tomatoes

$^1/_2$ cup chopped scallions, green parts only

$^1/_2$ cup finely chopped onion

1 tablespoon chopped fresh cilantro leaves

2 teaspoons freshly squeezed lemon juice

1 teaspoon salt

Freshly ground black pepper

Cut the tomatoes in half and squeeze the seeds out over a bowl. Coarsely chop them and add to the bowl with the seeds. Stir in the scallions, onions, and cilantro. Add the lemon juice, salt, and pepper to taste, and mix well. Cover and chill in the refrigerator for at least 30 minutes and up to 1 day. Remove from the refrigerator about 15 minutes before serving.

My Meaty Spaghetti Sauce

When you cook for many, as I do, you learn to improvise and create sauces and dishes that you know will go a long way; that was the inspiration behind my own spaghetti sauce. This isn't for the light eater. It's a hefty sauce (I have seven men in my home!) and as far as they're concerned, the meatier and thicker the better.

MAKE ABOUT 6 CUPS

3 tablespoons olive oil

1 medium onion, peeled and minced

4 garlic cloves, peeled and crushed

1 pound lean ground beef

1 pound Italian pork sausage links, removed from casing

One 28-ounce can tomato puree

1 tablespoon sugar

2 fresh basil leaves

1 bay leaf

1 teaspoon chopped fresh parsley

1 teaspoon fresh oregano or $1/2$ teaspoon dried

$1/2$ teaspoon salt

$1/2$ teaspoon freshly ground black pepper

1 Heat the oil in a heavy pot over medium heat. Add the onion and garlic and cook, stirring frequently, until the garlic is golden brown, about 3 minutes.

2 Add the beef and sausage and cook, stirring frequently, breaking up larger chunks with a wooden spoon, until the meat is cooked through and no longer pink, about 15 minutes.

3 Stir in the tomato puree, sugar, basil, bay leaf, parsley, oregano, salt, and pepper. Simmer until bubbling, about 10 minutes.

4 Serve immediately over your favorite pasta, or let cool, transfer to a glass or plastic container, cover, and refrigerate for up to 3 days, or freeze for up to 3 months. Remove bay leave serving.

NOTE: This sauce is great served as I did for my twins, Mark and Eric, when they were little—over spaghetti, with two 9-ounce cans of Vienna sausages (sautéed in a bit of olive oil to warm), and a teaspoon of Sofrito (page 158). The added touch of the sofrito to the sauce, along with the flavors of the sausages, is terrific!

My Best Barbecue Sauce

In my home, barbecue sauce is considered the "other ketchup" because my boys and I love it on anything: pork chops, chicken, even French fries! There's something about this tangy and sweet sauce that marries well with so many dishes—and you can make it ahead of time and keep it in your refrigerator for several weeks.

MAKES 1 CUP

$^1/_2$ cup light brown sugar

$^1/_4$ cup ketchup

$^1/_4$ cup freshly squeezed lime juice

3 tablespoons honey

$^1/_4$ cup chopped fresh cilantro leaves

2 garlic cloves, peeled and finely minced

1 splash white vinegar

1 tablespoon store-bought teriyaki sauce

$^1/_2$ teaspoon ground cumin

$^1/_2$ teaspoon ground nutmeg

Salt and freshly ground black pepper

In a medium saucepan over low heat, combine the sugar and $^1/_4$ cup water and cook, stirring constantly so it doesn't burn or stick. Once the sugar has dissolved, add the ketchup, lime juice, honey, cilantro, garlic, vinegar, teriyaki sauce, cumin, and nutmeg, stirring constantly. Add salt and pepper to taste and remove from the heat. Taste and adjust as needed; if it's too thick, add a bit more water. Use immediately, or let cool to room temperature, transfer to a glass or plastic container, cover, and refrigerate for up to 3 weeks.

Mexican-Style Corn

When Nicholas was a baby, he had a fabulous Mexican babysitter, Estela. Not only did she treat my youngest with great tenderness and love, she also taught me a lot about cooking. I remember she was there one night when I was making my usual white rice, and she asked me, "*¿No te gusta el maíz?*" (Don't you like corn?). She went on to teach me how to make her style of corn, and how it could jazz up my rice or be eaten as a side dish. Try serving this on its own, or mixed into Basic White Rice (page 171). If you have any left over, you can also sprinkle it cold on top of a salad of mixed greens; the corn adds a small sweet touch to so many dishes.

SERVES 4 TO 6 AS A SIDE DISH (MAKES ABOUT 2¹/₂ CUPS)

3 tablespoons unsalted butter

2 cups fresh or frozen corn kernels

2 tablespoons seeded and finely chopped green bell pepper

2 tablespoons seeded and finely chopped red bell pepper

1 teaspoon salt

Freshly ground black pepper

1 tablespoon chopped fresh cilantro leaves

In a medium saucepan, melt the butter over medium-low heat. Add the corn, peppers, salt, and pepper to taste. Cook, stirring occasionally to keep the corn from browning, until heated through, 5 to 8 minutes. Top with the cilantro and serve.

Pickled Cabbage

The first time I tried this was in Ray's mom's home. I glanced into a small white bowl, and saw the cabbage soaking, and immediately assumed it was some kind of salad in the process of being prepared. I soon learned that that was it! Served alongside Arroz con Habichuelas Rosadas (page 98), this lightly pickled cabbage offers the perfect flavor and textural counterbalance. Serve with any of my rice dishes, or any pork or chicken dish.

SERVES 4

$^1/_2$ head white cabbage, about $^1/_2$ pound, not cored

$^1/_4$ cup white vinegar (or more, according to taste)

Salt and freshly ground black pepper

Use a sharp knife to carefully shred the cabbage into long thin pieces. Transfer to a salad bowl. Pour the vinegar on top, along with enough water to cover the cabbage. Add salt and pepper to taste and mix well. Cover and let this rest for at least 10 minutes or up to a day. Use a fork or slotted spoon to remove the cabbage from the liquid and serve.

Basic White Rice

As in many cultures throughout the world, rice is a key staple in Puerto Rican family-style cooking. Here's my basic recipe. I also use a sheet of aluminum foil under my *caldero* lid, just to make sure it's well sealed.

**SERVES 6 TO 8
(MAKES 6 CUPS)**

Salt

1/4 cup vegetable oil

2 cups white rice

1 Pour 4 cups water into a *caldero* or heavy pot, add a few pinches of salt, and bring to a boil. Add the oil. Meanwhile, rinse the rice in a fine-mesh strainer with lukewarm water (this gets rid some of the starch).

2 Carefully taste the water; you should be able to taste the salt. If not, add more. Add the rice. Cook uncovered over medium heat, until the rice has absorbed most of the water, about 5 minutes.

3 Cover and cook over low heat until the rice is tender, 12 to 15 minutes.

4 Remove the lid, and test the consistency of rice. If it's too hard, cover again and cook until it's tender; it shouldn't take more than another 5 or 10 minutes. Serve immediately.

Garlic Bread

When you've got seven boys (including Ray!) you realize you have some hefty appetites to deal with. Of course, I try to plan accordingly, but sometimes my amounts are off, and I need just a bit more of something to get them to the finish line; that's why I always have some Italian bread or rolls handy. I'll take Italian or French bread, season it, and serve it with meals to my very welcoming audience.

SERVES 8 TO 10

Nonstick cooking spray

2 loaves Italian bread or 1 French baguette
(the Italian bread I buy is usually a little longer than 12 inches; the French baguette would be longer)

4 tablespoons ($^1/_2$ stick) unsalted butter, softened enough to spread easily

2 cloves fresh garlic, crushed

1 teaspoon garlic salt

$^1/_2$ teaspoon chopped fresh parsley leaves

Freshly grated Parmesan cheese

1 Preheat the oven to 325°F.

2 Line a baking sheet with aluminum foil and coat with cooking spray (or a little butter) so the bread won't stick.

3 Slice the bread lengthwise down the middle. Spread the butter on the cut side of the bread and sprinkle with the garlic, followed by the garlic salt. Place, open side up, on the prepared baking sheet and bake until the bread is light brown, about 15 minutes.

4 Cut into quarters or thirds, sprinkle the parsley and Parmesan on top, and serve.

Drinks

One of my key rules for life is that you've got to enjoy it; for this reason, I think that we busy parents always need to make time for ourselves! These simple party-style drinks are great for grown-up relaxation. My philosophy for creating cocktails is similar to that of creating meals: Drinks should be quick, easy, and packed with punch and *mucho amor*! Drinks should complement the meals they accompany. A tall glass of sangría is great on any festive occasion; strawberry daiquiris are always tasty, gorgeous, and fun, and *coquito* can be a great beginning—or ending. Most of the drinks in this section have been handed down to me over the course of many years, traditional fiestas, and *celebraciones*. So lift up your glass and say, *¡Salud!*

Coquito *Puerto Rican Eggnog*

Coquito is Puerto Rico's winter holiday drink. Served mostly around Christmas and New Year's—but also at Thanksgiving—this drink has become synonymous with the holidays. Like most Puerto Ricans, I can't imagine a Christmas without coquito! Mercedes, Ray's mom, says the easiest way to prepare this is to combine all the ingredients in a big bowl. Once it's properly mixed, you can pour it into empty gallon bottles and refrigerate it for up to 1 week. In fact, it gets better with time! (Of course, this is not a recipe for people with reduced immune systems, who should avoid raw eggs—I'm sorry!)

**SERVES ABOUT 8
(MAKES ¹/₂ GALLON)**

Once 15-ounce can cream of coconut (I prefer Coco Lopez)

¹/₂ quart eggnog (store-bought or your favorite recipe)

Half a 12-ounce can evaporated milk

3 cinnamon sticks

¹/₂ cup sugar

3 large egg yolks (discard the whites or save them for another use)

¹/₂ a fifth (12.5 ounces) dark rum (or more)

1 Combine the cream of coconut, eggnog, and milk in a bowl and set aside in the refrigerator.

2 In a sauce pan over medium heat, combine 1 cups water and cinnamon sticks, bring to a soft boil, and let simmer until the water turns brown, about 5 minutes. Reduce the heat to low, and slowly add the sugar, whisking to help dissolve it quickly. Let simmer until it reaches a syrupy consistency, about 10 minutes. Remove it from the heat, and let cool to room temperature.

3 Using a wire whisk, whisk the yolks well in a very large bowl until they're thoroughly mixed, about 5 minutes. Add the cream of coconut mixture, cinnamon syrup, and rum and mix well. Taste it and add more rum according to your liking.

4 Transfer to a clean half-gallon bottle and refrigerate for at least 1 hour, or up to 1 week. Shake to recombine if necessary and remove the cinnamon sticks just before serving.

Piña Colada

Every time I visit Ray's mom, she's not only prepared to serve me a feast, but also to offer me fabulous cocktails! For years she has made me great piña coladas, and though I tried to make them like hers, something seemed to be missing. Then finally I figured it out. I noticed that Mercedes always kept her cans of pineapple juice and cream of coconut in the freezer; she never uses ice to make her frozen drinks. This is a great technique because the flavors are never watered down. Serve these luscious drinks any time, with Tostones (page 74), Bacalaítos (page 62), or your favorite snack.

SERVES 4

Half a 46-ounce can pineapple juice (I prefer Dole)

One 15-ounce can cream of coconut (I prefer Coco Lopez)

1 cup light rum (I prefer Bacardi; you can change the amount depending on your mood!)

1. Freeze the juice and cream of coconut overnight. When you're ready to make the piña coladas, take them out of the freezer and let them thaw until they're slightly softened, about 30 minutes.

2. In a blender, combine the partially frozen juice and cream of coconut with the rum. Blend and serve immediately.

Sangría de Soco

The first time Ray and I took a trip to Puerto Rico together, it was to meet his oldest brother Ramón and his wife, Socorro. The aroma of her cooking invited me in; she greeted us with sangría she had prepared and chilled before our arrival. Soco, as we affectionately call her, made sangría that was quite different from the kind I was used to (she didn't add any fresh fruit), but I enjoyed its intense flavor— and its punch! (This is her recipe, only when I make it, I add fresh pineapple or orange slices. Other than that, I wouldn't change any other part of Soco's Sangría!) She made this two-gallon mixture in a big *caldero* (rice pot), then poured the mix into two clean, empty gallon milk containers, to store in the refrigerator. You can always double the recipe to make more for a larger crowd, or for a gathering on the following day!

**SERVES 16 TO 20
(MAKES 1 GALLON)**

1 gallon Burgundy wine (she uses Gallo)

1 quart orange juice

$1/2$ liter vodka or light rum

$1^1/_2$ 11.5- to 12-ounce cans frozen concentrated grape juice (she uses Welch's)

$1^1/_2$ 12-ounce cans frozen concentrated pineapple juice (she uses Dole)

Juice from 1 lemons

About 10 pineapple wedges or thin orange slices for garnish

Combine all the ingredients except the fresh fruit in a large container. Mix well. Pour into smaller containers as desired. Chill for at least 4 hours, and up to 1 week. Add fresh fruit just before serving.

Café con Kahlúa

After we spent the night at my sister Melissa's house following a News Year's Eve bash, I woke up looking for my *café*; it had been a long night! We gathered around the table with our coffees. Mel pulled out her bottle of Kahlúa, and we started the party—all over again! Since then, I've served this drink after many dinners in my home. The Kahlúa, or any coffee liqueur, will add flavor, sweetness, and kick to your favorite coffee.

SERVES 4

El Pico or other Latin-style ground coffee

Milk (optional)

$^1/_2$ cup Kahlúa or your favorite coffee liqueur

Brew a small pot of coffee. When it's ready, fill serving cups about three-fourths of the way with it. Add milk, if that's the way you like it, but don't add sugar, because the liqueur will sweeten it. Add an ounce of coffee liqueur and serve.

Limoncillo   *Lemonade Cocktail*

Maybe *limoncillo* (literally, little lemon) is a cousin of *limoncello*, the Italian lemon liqueur, which is served well chilled during steamy summer months! They're both very refreshing, light, sweet, and tasty. We were introduced to limoncillo during a visit from Ray's niece. She and her husband were staying with us during one incredibly hot summer. We arrived home from work one day, and discovered that not only had they surprised us by painting our fence, they had also prepared us their favorite *refresco* (refreshment)! Since then, I regularly make limoncillo to enjoy during summer-time barbecues, as well as when I felt like serving (and drinking!) something really light.

SERVES 4

Ice

1 cup light rum (I prefer Bacardi)

2 cups of your favorite lemonade

4 lemon twists

Fill four tall glasses with ice. Pour $1/4$ cup of the rum into each glass. Top with $1/2$ cup of the lemonade. Stir well (using a bar stirrer— or a chopstick!), garnish with a lemon twist, and serve.

Frozen Guava Margarita

Guavas are not only wonderfully fragrant and tasty, their seductive flavor—even combined with neighbor Mexico's alcohol—will make any Puerto Rican yearn for a visit back to the island! This cocktail promises summer on even the dampest and darkest winter day. Thanks to Ray's mom, I've learned that freezing guava juice ahead of time makes for much fruitier—and less ice-diluted—cocktails. I recommend preparing these margaritas, putting on some salsa music, and having some fun—any time! Serve with Tostones (page 74) or Arañitas (page 75).

SERVES 4

4 cups guava nectar (I prefer Libby's or Kern's Guava Nectar)

$^1/_2$ cup silver tequila

2 tablespoons fresh lime juice

1 tablespoon triple sec

Coarse salt (optional)

4 lime slices for garnish

1. The day before you plan to serve, fill two ice trays with the guava nectar and let them freeze overnight.

2. In a blender, combine the frozen guava cubes with the tequila, lime juice, and triple sec and process until smooth.

3. If you're like me, you like your margaritas with salt—simply pour about $^1/_4$ cup of coarse salt onto a small flat plate, dampen the rims of the glasses with a lime wedge, and gently place them in the salt to coat the rim.

4. Pour the guava-tequila mixture into the glasses, garnish with lime slices, and serve immediately, or let sit in the freezer (for some extra chill!) for 10 minutes before serving.

Elsie's Turkey Tacos and Arroz con Pollo

Strawberry Daiquiris

Ray's mom, Mercedes, is a fan of sweet beverages. Whenever we take her out to dinner, she requests either sweet wine, a piña colada, or another one of her favorite cocktails: a strawberry daiquiri. I enjoy these delightfully refreshing (and deceptively sweet!) cocktails as much on steamy summer days as on winter days when I yearn for sun. Like Mercedes, I've learned to keep frozen strawberries—and *crema de coco* (cream of coconut)—ready in my freezer and rum, of course, in my cabinet. Serve with Yuca Frita (page 78), Guanimes de Maíz (page 80), or whatever snack you're in the mood for!

SERVES 4

One 16-ounce package frozen whole unsweetened strawberries
1 cup light rum (I prefer Bacardi)
2 teaspoons frozen cream of coconut (I prefer Coco Lopez)

In a blender, combine the strawberries, rum, and cream of coconut. Blend and serve immediately.

Index

Elsie's Turkey Tacos and Arroz con Pollo